In Pursuit of 'Normal'

In Pursuit of 'Normal'

Martha Siede

atmosphere press

To Sophie,
This book would not have been written without your
input and encouragement.

Please be advised that this book discusses:

Medical details
Suicide
Infertility
Sexual references
Female weight

Table of Contents

PART 3: Life's Reflections

PART 1

LIFE'S INTERRUPTIONS

Chapter 1

Coma

To Relax into a State of Nothingness

I was being propelled forward, on what I thought was a trolley, down a corridor with familiar rectangular shapes on the ceiling.

I awoke to see a man standing above my head. He wore a blue gown, cap, and a face mask.

The room was harshly lit. The walls around me were stark and sterile. The sounds of footsteps and wheels turning echoed off the walls as I was moved forward.

The air was cold and I could smell a distinct scent of cleanliness familiar to me.

The blue silhouette had broad, square shoulders; that of a man.

Realising I was awake, a calm, firm voice said, "We are going to sedate you and put you in an induced coma."

I felt relieved.

I wanted to relax, let my muscles loosen, and have a warmth wash over me. I could not wait to abandon my body. I was exhausted. To be put into an effortless state of sleep sounded like heaven.

As my eyes closed, everything went dark, and the harrowing hallucinations began...

I say 'hallucinations,' but what I encountered in my mind was a jumble of dreams and reality. Reality consisted of what was happening around me and on the television in my room.

My mind never stopped while I was in a coma. A constant reel of never-ending scenes bombarded my mind with intense emotions that remained with me long after I woke.

The hallucinations went on for sixty-seven days.

Some hallucinations had me offering myself to die. I felt like I had been held hostage in a hospital and I had to submit to get out. Sometimes I questioned if I was in a hospital, seeing that there were no doors or windows to look out.

The constant barrage of images and emotions was so intense that I felt exhausted. I was fighting for my life the whole time I was in my coma.

My mind was not the only thing fighting to keep me alive. So was my body.

It was August 2021, at the start of the Delta wave of the COVID-19 pandemic.

My right hip was sore, as it had been for the past two years; it had incrementally gotten worse to the point where the pain had become unbearable.

When drugs no longer helped, I finally succumbed to seeing a surgeon, as my hip was not going to recover by itself. I had tried physiotherapy, which made my pain worse. I had seen an osteopath, which marginally helped.

The surgeon's office had a large frame of four photos of his beautiful daughters on the wall above his desk.

"Four beautiful daughters! How lucky are you?"

The surgeon was of Egyptian descent, probably in his late mid-sixties. He had a calm, reassuring voice, a grey beard, a bald head, and an average height and build.

"You have worn a hole in the top of your hip, which explains the pain you are in. Every movement we make involves our hip, so the pain is not escaping. Can you walk?"

"No, I've never walked."

He told me I would need an operation and I would "be back home in three days."

The surgeon sounded confident but I should have been more cautious, looking back. There were other patients in his waiting room chatting to each other about their body parts still being sore — a pain in the shoulder and a knee that still hurt even after their surgery.

I later learned that my surgeon did not specialise in hips. He is a Jack-of-all-trades, operating on hips, shoulders, knees, and other joints.

I did not know some surgeons just specialised in operating on hips. I trusted my GP, a General Practitioner (Doctor), to refer me to a good surgeon who would do their best to fix me. I was in no state to be picky as I was in level fifteen out of ten pain.

My operation was set for three weeks after I met the surgeon.

I live with Andrew, my husband of twenty-one years. Andrew is fifty years old and looks the opposite of me. He has dark blond hair and blue eyes. Andrew is a fifth-generation Aussie with the fairest of skin. He is tall and of a slim build.

I fell in love with Andrew not because of his fashion sense, but because Andrew is serious, sensible, and intelligent with a heart of gold. He is loyal, caring, and very wise. Andrew is my rock. He is not going anywhere as he does not change his mind quickly, and I can lean on him.

I have brown eyes, brown hair, and olive skin, and I am short, although you would not know when looking at me. As I always sit down, I have relatively long legs and a short torso. My olive skin comes from my Maltese parents.

I sit down a lot because I use a wheelchair to get around. I have cerebral palsy, which was caused by a lack of oxygen just after I was born. My birth was somewhat unconventional. I was born bottom-first. My Mum struggled to push me out for over twenty-four hours; I should have been delivered via caesarean, but I was not. It took doctors forty minutes to revive me fully.

We live with our three dogs, Pupa, Bronte, and Pixie. Pupa and Bronte are full sisters and are maltalier, a mixed breed of Maltese and cavalier. Pixie is a crossbreed of Maltese and Australian silky. I often tell Andrew that if he and I had a child, the child would look like Pixie — cute!

We live in a brick veneer home in Western Sydney, where I grew up. Our home is very spacious. The kitchen is in the middle of the house. We have three bedrooms, a formal lounge and dining, a family room and eating area, two bathrooms, and a laundry. We have a double-car garage that will only ever fit one car as Andrew has lots of tools and 'man stuff.'

Two of our three bedrooms are our offices. Andrew and I have an office each. Mine is the tidy, stylish one, and Andrew's is, let's say, chaotic and full!

When the COVID-19 Delta wave hit, I asked Mum to come and stay with us. Mum could not get food and other supplies for herself while we were all in lockdown as she did not drive. I thought it would be convenient for her to stay with us, and because Andrew could drive, he could get our supplies.

Mum is eighty years old. She now has grey hair; when she was young, her hair was dark brown. Mum has green eyes, olive skin, and is short. Mum grew up with a slender build until the middle-age spread happened.

Since we do not have a 'spare' bedroom, Mum sleeps in the lounge when she comes to stay.

A week after meeting the surgeon, my right leg was not supporting me very well at all.

For me to get off my wheelchair and onto the floor, I had to brace myself. It was excruciatingly painful. I started falling to the floor whenever I tried to get onto the toilet. It felt like my heart was in my throat all the time due to the pain. I felt a stabbing, sharp pain, like my hip bone was going to come out through my waist.

Even standing up and holding onto the railing in the bathroom was excruciating, as was sitting on the floor and lying in bed. The only place I was comfortable was sitting in my wheelchair.

To sleep at night, I lay on my side in bed with my legs bent up like I was seated.

The pain got so intense one night that I begged Andrew to call an ambulance.

The paramedics introduced me to the 'green whistle.' The green whistle is a medical device that looks like a whistle that administers a fast-acting pain medication called Penthrox through an inhaler for immediate pain relief. By sucking on the mouthpiece, the medicine is inhaled and takes away the pain...Well, it is meant to, but my pain continued. My pain was extreme and the surgery was still two weeks away. They sent me home with some extra-strong pain medication.

Forty-eight hours later, I was in the same predicament but rang an ambulance myself this time.

The hospital admitted me and three days later I had surgery.

The surgery went on for three hours. In recovery, I remember being told that I had to press a button for pain relief every five minutes. I asked Andrew to press the button because I could not focus enough to push it myself. I have no memory of that night, but I was told I was very restless and that Andrew hardly slept because I was up and down throughout the night.

When I eventually settled, I began to lose consciousness. Andrew told the nurses that something was wrong. My blood pressure had dropped and my heart rate was fast.

It was a long night and an even longer day for Andrew. I had lost consciousness and I was transferred to the high-dependency ward on Wednesday, 11th August 2021. Andrew was sent home to get some rest.

At 6am the following day, an intensive care unit doctor rang Andrew to say that I had been taken back into surgery to investigate why I had low blood pressure and a high pulse rate.

The doctors discovered that I had a fractured pelvis and blood had pooled into my buttock. The fracture occurred during the hip operation. I was given several blood transfusions.

I had lost so much blood from my body that my kidneys shut down. I was put on kidney dialysis because I had stopped producing urine. Our kidneys remove waste and extra fluid from our body through urine. When we lose a lot of blood, our kidneys can shrink and stop working. That is what happened to me.

On Thursday, 12th August 2021, I was transferred to the ICU, bloated from my kidneys shutting down, sedated on a ventilator, with wires and tubes going into and out of my body to do various medical things. I looked like I had been in an accident, not recovering from a hip replacement.

The ICU medical team tried to wake me from my coma twice. The first time I remember seeing bright lights, a wave of heat washing through my body, and a feeling of anxiety. I was fighting hard to breathe. Then it was all over. I did not know if what I was experiencing was real or an hallucination.

The second time they tried to wake me, I lasted a shorter time awake as I did not try to breathe for myself at all. I told myself that if I did not fight to breathe, the hallucination would be over quickly. This concerned the medical team as I was no longer fighting for myself.

The mind is a fascinating tool that tries to make the best out of all dire circumstances.

My niece, Leeanne, the daughter of my eldest sister, Ruth, is ten years younger than me, with blonde hair and brown eyes. She is a doer. Leeanne fell into the position of being my advocate, talking to doctors, fighting with them to not give up on me and to keep trying to bring me out of my coma.

Leeanne told the doctors that I had responded well to Mum visiting me when I was a sick baby and that this could help me wake up.

A month after being in a coma, Andrew and Mum were

given special permission to visit me. The doctors felt that they had done everything they could for me and I was not progressing. The next step was to keep me sedated and put me in a nursing home. My family said, "That is never going to happen."

On the first visit, the doctors looked to see how my vital signs responded to the family contact. I responded well, and once Andrew and Mum got home they received a call asking them to visit me the next day as the doctors were so happy with my improvements.

It was then decided that Andrew and Mum could visit twice a week, and later, Leeanne could visit once a week.

I kept improving with each visit from Andrew, Mum, and Leeanne. In the month following the first visit, my sedation was incrementally brought down and I slowly woke up in my own time.

Having family in the room to love and touch you is paramount to waking from a coma. Seeing them via video was never enough. My Mum has superpowers in person!

In Pursuit...

- Pain is not something anyone wants to live with or tolerate. When we are in pain, we hope it passes. In hindsight, I would have sought help earlier and stopped trying so hard to manage the pain.

- Tapping into a coma patient's mind to align what is happening could be helpful.

- Our mind is the only thing that can keep us alive when left in the care of strangers.

- Our family fighting for us helps us stay alive.

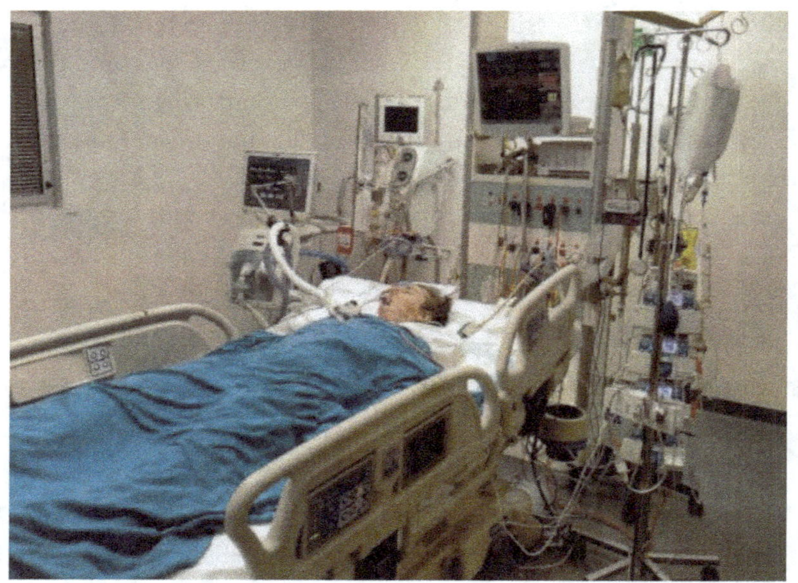

In a coma

Chapter 2

After I Woke Up

Reality Blurs into Dreams and Vice Versa until the Sedation Wears Off

Waking up from a coma takes time. I drifted in and out of consciousness for days.

I was not fully awake, as I do not remember much of the first week.

When I became lucid, I could not talk, as I had a trachea, and I had this thing that looked like a chicken bone sticking out of my nose. It was my feeding tube and not a bone that grew out of my nose while I slept!

I remember the nurses kept repeating that I had been in a coma, I could not talk right now, and that I was going to be okay.

Communication was challenging as I had no muscle tone in my arms, so I could not write. The lack of muscle meant I had no gross or fine motor skills to keep my finger pointing at letters on a board or typing on a phone to communicate.

My only communication was nodding 'yes' or shaking my head 'no.' People had to ask me questions in a yes/no format.

Andrew was the only person who could read my lips, which was terrific. Andrew has a slight form of autism and does not usually look at my face when I speak. The fact that he could look at me and decipher what I said was a relief.

I vaguely remember asking Andrew to bring me my wheelchair and a list of clothes I needed.

Very slowly, I learned to breathe on my own, and the trachea was taken out. I then learned to drink and eat thickened liquids. I got into trouble with the speech therapist for mixing the green drink I had been prescribed with ice to water it down. The lime drink tasted strong, but he told me this would have been a choking hazard.

Clint, my speech therapist, had blue eyes and shoulder-length red hair that he wore in a ponytail. I asked Clint to show me his face without a mask. He had a lovely face. Clint knew his stuff and was fun to work with. Slowly, with the help of Clint, I learned to drink liquids again.

One day, Clint made me a cup of tea, the worst cup I had ever had. Our in-joke about Clint was that it was lucky he had a lovely face because he could not make a nice cup of tea to save his life!

I have been drinking tea since I was five, so I know a good cuppa when I taste one.

The proper way to make tea using a tea bag is to pop your tea bag into a cup, pour slightly boiling water over the bag, let the bag steep for three to five minutes, then pull the bag out; do not squeeze it; put in sugar and stir; put in the milk. That is how a nice cup of tea is made.

I had to learn to drink slowly so that I did not aspirate and have the liquid go down my windpipe and into my lungs. Aspirating could have done a lot of damage to my windpipe and lungs if the liquid had gone down the wrong way. Fortunately, I had a strong enough cough to expel any liquids that went down that way.

Clint also had me try eating a shortbread cream biscuit; after the first bite, I exclaimed, "I am not ready to eat this." At that point, he was happy that I knew my limitations.

My meals consisted of pureed foods. My favourite meal was breakfast, where I had canned spaghetti. I kept this breakfast for about six months after leaving the hospital. The rest of my meals were pureed mac and cheese and pureed ravioli. I was not gaining weight in any hurry.

Before I went in for my hip operation, I was fifty-five kilos. When I woke up from the coma, I was forty-four kilos. In one week of eating, I had only put on one hundred grams, so they kept tube-feeding me as well.

I worked with Fiona, the physiotherapist, a middle-aged lady with curly brown hair, brown eyes, and a solid build. Fiona had strong ideas and wanted me to do things her way.

Fiona worked with me to get out of bed, into my wheel-chair, and back onto the bed.

The first time I had to move out of bed, I freaked out because I could not move my right leg. My right leg had been immobilised for a long time so that my right hip could heal after the hip replacement, and all the muscles had wasted away. They call it atrophy. There is a saying, 'Use it or lose it.'

I freaked out because my right leg was my good leg. I cannot function if my right leg is not working. My right leg is the one that does all the hard work; it is reliable and does what I ask it to do most of the time.

My left leg is unreliable. At times, it tries to fight me when I ask it to do anything and, without notice, will stop holding me up by flexing up or kicking out — an involuntary move-ment or a spasm.

When I told Fiona my right leg was not working, she responded, "It's okay, you can use your left leg." I did not have a voice, so I could not explain how my body worked. I just nodded. I thought, in time, my body would show her its menacing ways.

I worked with Fiona on sitting up and hanging my legs over the side of the bed. I needed a lot of help with this as I had no muscles to move my body around, and I could not sit up as all the muscles had wasted away in my stomach and back. Just being sat up caused me dizziness and nausea. After sitting up for a minute, I would have to lie down again.

During the day, I was given exercises to help me flex my hands and arms, as well as my ankles and legs.

My second eldest sister, Esther, and I look very similar. Esther has brown eyes and hair, olive skin, and a slender build. Esther and I are close and can thrash out ideas with each other. I remember talking to Esther about how I could not understand what you had to do to sit up. It was like the mechanics of it all were beyond my comprehension.

Things clicked after my conversation with Esther about how frustrated I was, and I started sitting alone. Something happens in the brain where if you speak a problem out or write about it, the problem moves to the other side of your brain and can be worked out. It took me over a month to sit up on my own again and over a year to gain enough strength in my torso to not lose my balance when I was sitting or crawling on the floor.

After learning to sit up enough that I was not dizzy or did not feel like I was going to vomit, Fiona worked with me on transfers, where I moved from one surface to another — for example, bed to wheelchair. Using a transfer board to do this is scary. It is kind of like asking someone with dystonic cerebral palsy to walk a tightrope.

I have dystonic cerebral palsy, which was caused by a lack of oxygen to my brain, causing brain damage. My disability comes under the cerebral palsy umbrella. The dystonic part means I have involuntary movements that cause havoc with my balance and coordination.

The idea of having a solid board shaped like a kidney placed across from bed to wheelchair, having to slide on it from one side to the other, was sickening. I was so opposed to it because of my involuntary movements. I was scared the board would fly forward if I spasmed and leaned back.

The board is placed under my buttocks, and the aim is to slide towards my destination — in this case, the wheelchair. To make this process easier, the bed is elevated higher than the wheelchair to send me in a downward direction, to ease the transfer by moving my feet towards the wheelchair; I used my arms to slide my body towards the chair. I keep doing this until I arrive in the wheelchair and pull the board from under me. If everything goes to plan, I am now in the wheelchair, and I wait for the nausea to subside.

I did not use the board very much because I thought it was unsafe. Being stood up and swivelled around to sit in my wheelchair was a safer way to achieve the transfer.

The first time I was in my wheelchair after my coma, I was taken outside onto the balcony, where there were plants and flowers to look at. Accompanying me on this trek to the balcony was an oxygen tank, a heart rate monitor, a urine bag, a nurse, a physiotherapist, and an occupational therapist. It was a massive job. I felt like I had an entourage with extras.

A comment was made that my urine looked good. I did not understand why that comment was made then. It was not until later that I learned that my kidneys had shut down due to the significant blood loss that occurred when my pelvis was broken. When your kidneys shut down, you stop producing urine and you need dialysis to get rid of the waste your body produces. I had dialysis for over two months every couple of days. My family was told that I may need dialysis three times a week for the rest of my life. My church prayed that my kidneys would be healed, and they were, and I started producing urine again. I believe that members of my church family prayed explicitly that I would not need dialysis, and the prayer was answered, and I was healed. No dialysis was required after I woke up from the ICU.

It took a while to comprehend everything that happened to me. I am still learning what everything means and the impact it has on things like constipation and coughing up mucus.

I thought I had been eating incorrectly, but the truth is that my body needs time to heal and be right again. As I write this, I feel that I have the constipation under control, and my system is working as it should. However, stress or a change of scene can upset things again. It is a daily process, and I am always very grateful when my system works.

Not having dialysis explained to me and the ramifications of having had my kidneys shut down is very frustrating. I have had to figure out a lot of what is wrong with my body and why on my own. More information needed to be given to me before I left the hospital.

Seeing life below me on the balcony was lovely: cars driving past, people walking around, and construction work happening. I was able to make peace with the hallucination of not knowing what hospital I was in. I could see that I was in my local hospital.

I did not stay on the balcony very long as I got tired quickly, so we made the trek back to my room and onto my bed. I then slept for a while to recover. Once I started to gain some strength, I started wheeling myself to the balcony. Tens of metres led to one hundred metres, all the way out to the balcony.

While I was in ICU, every day would be another trek onto the balcony. I could stay for extended periods; Andrew would sometimes join us and we would even eat lunch there.

The weather was slowly getting warmer, as it was now October. I needed a jacket and leggings, but the sun was lovely. I loved letting the sun warm my face and looking at all the flowers and plants God had created. The intricacies of it all.

The slide board was still a menace, but I conquered it well enough that Fiona, the physiotherapist, was happy.

My daily routine was going out onto the balcony and doing physiotherapy in bed. I moved my arms and legs, hands and feet.

After a couple of days of being able to get into my wheelchair, the ICU staff decided that it was time for me to have a shower.

My first shower chair was nice and soft, which was great because, being a bag of skin and bone, I needed some cushioning.

The bathroom was huge and had no heating. The nurses wet me down with the shower, and because I was wet and there was a draft; my limbs became very stiff. They washed my hair and my body. Dried me and dressed me. It was a shock to the system to be that cold and stiff. I was tired at the end of that shower. Back in bed, I was covered with warm blankets and slept for a few hours. That ordeal took everything out of me and I had to recover.

I did not have a hoist at home, so they used a metal shower chair for my next shower that could be moved closer to the bed to transfer onto using the transfer board.

The metal shower chair was awful. Because I had lost so much weight, there was no padding on my bottom or back, and it was excruciating to sit on metal and plastic. My body spasmed, and I could not sit still enough and be safe. I asked for towels on the seat and behind my back to give me some padding. I asked for each area of my body they would wash to be wet, cleaned, and then dried so I remained warm.

The nurse first wet my hair and face, washed them, dried them, and then my torso, arms, and legs. This showering process was kinder on my body, kept me warmer, and allowed me to recover quicker.

I only had showers when I needed to wash my hair. Otherwise, I used 'bath in bed' wipes.

When I got home, I used my old wheelchair to shower as it could support me while I was in the shower and give me greater comfort. After about four to five months at home, I transitioned back to sitting on the floor and showering.

The floor is my safe place. You cannot fall any further than the floor.

I stayed in ICU for a lot longer than I needed to, as no ward wanted to take me on.

As I continued to recover in the ICU, I had a nurse who was taking care of two patients instead of just me. My family had been advocating against this as I always needed one-on-one care. I slipped down the bed, twisting my right hip, and I freaked out. The nurse was busy with the other patient, and I had to stay in that position for about thirty minutes until a wardsman could attend.

Before I left the ICU, an older male nurse, John, came in and shared that he had been a nurse for over thirty years and had not experienced many miracles, but that I was one of them. Wow!

There had to be a meeting to move me to a ward.

A Zoom meeting was held with the physiotherapist, occupational therapist, ICU social worker, ward social worker, doctors, other family members, Andrew, and me to discuss my need to move to a ward. A member of my family or a nurse needed to stay with me the whole time because of the severity of my needs, which were now made worse by having no voice and no muscles. The people in the room did not want to listen or understand. It did not matter how much my family advocated for me or saw the state I was in. They saw it as unnecessary to have a person with me twenty-four-seven.

People with disabilities generally have a different healthcare experience from their counterparts without disability. There's a health gap between people with disabilities and those without. There's a difference in life expectancy. [1]

No one wants to take on a patient with physical disabilities and extraordinary, albeit realistic, demands from her family. The ward certainly did not want me.

I was eventually moved to the west ward. Andrew was permitted to stay with me from 8am to 8pm, and a nurse

---

1 Palipana, Dinesh, 2022, Stronger - How losing everything set me free, Macmillan, Australia, page 98.

would be with me one-on-one for the other twelve hours. Jess, a nurse in her first year of training, was provided on the first night I was there. The second night, Andrew and I waited for the nurse to arrive. We were told no nurse was coming as they were short-staffed. I had anxiety, as I did not want to be alone, especially at night in the dark. Andrew was made to go home. I felt trapped, unable to call for help when needed, and had trouble pressing the call button.

The following day, the nurse manager moved me to a room closer to the nurse's station. This room was no better, as I was still out of eyeshot from the nurse's station. The room was dark and I had massive anxiety as it reminded me of my ICU room. I refused to stay and wanted to be taken back to my other room with the big window where I could see the sky and the world outside.

I was moved back to my room, and I relaxed. As 8pm drew near, I had another anxiety attack as I did not want Andrew to leave. I started vomiting. I could not understand why I was having such an adverse reaction to Andrew having to leave.

Not much was said, but a mattress was brought for Andrew to stay the night. From that night on, Andrew stayed and looked after me. Mum would come for Andrew to take a few hours off and go home occasionally.

I learned later that patients who have been in a coma often experience anxiety attacks after they wake up when they feel vulnerable. I was feeling vulnerable because I was weak and uncoordinated. I felt much like a baby would, but I had an adult mind that could think.

The nursing staff thought Andrew would sit around and do nothing. They made him an 'honorary nurse' once they saw he was there to help me. As always, Andrew did an excellent job of looking after me. Nurses had to come in to give me my medications, attend to my dressings, and take my vitals. Andrew did the rest. The toileting, dressing, feeding, propping me up, and helping me with anything I needed.

We were always happy and polite, and the staff enjoyed working with us. I wish that they had just listened and heard my needs without it being such a battle. I am the one with the disability, and I know what I need. My family also knows my support needs and how to assist me.

It amazes me that hospitals cannot see a person in need and allow their family to do what they do for their loved one day in and day out in a hospital setting, especially when the patient has become so fragile and in need of that care. It is the care that nurses do not have the time to do because they are so busy looking after patients with a patient ratio that is too high.

Once in the ward, I started working with my physiotherapists, Johan and Catherine. Johan grew up in South Africa and liked using the pronunciation of his African name, Yohaan. He was tall, lanky, and fair. His hair was very short. He was a character that made you laugh all the time.

Catherine was also fair, with long hair in a braid. Catherine was quiet and a great listener. She was practical and a great problem-solver. Catherine helped me refine my 'getting out of bed' routine many times, making it more manageable. Our work together consisted of sitting up out of bed, sitting up independently for more extended periods, moving in and out of bed and onto my wheelchair, wheeling around, and then strengthening my arms three times a day by having exercise bands tied to the bed that I pulled with my arms.

Waking from my coma, my hands were sore, and I could not close them all the way or grab anything and hold it. The nerves in my hands were screaming in pain. When I got out of ICU and onto the ward, I was given Lyrica (pregabalin), a medication that helps with nerve pain. As the dose was increased, my hands felt a lot better, and I could close them all the way and grab and hold things without the searing pain. Later, when I saw my neurophysiologist, he recommended I increase the dose further to help reduce the spasms in my body.

In the coma, a considerable pressure ulcer developed on my heel. A pressure ulcer occurs when a patient is in one position for an extended period. Blood circulation is cut off and the surrounding tissue dies. In my case, I had a stage four pressure ulcer that impacted my skin, ligaments, tissue, and bone. For the first forty-eight years of my life, I had never had a pressure ulcer, and here I was in the hospital, waking up with a giant whopper on my heel. How was it never seen when bathing me? When I awoke, the nurses discovered the sore on my heel. I managed it, kept the pressure off, and ensured it healed. I was furious at this. It never hurt while healing, but once it healed, it was very tender to touch or to have on the ground without padding.

Treating my heel so it had the best chance of healing involved having it cleaned and covered in Betadine daily. Once I got out of the hospital, I had to have dressings every day for three months. A community nurse would call in the morning to check that I had no COVID-19 symptoms, then tell me they would be there during the day. There was a lot of waiting for the nurse to come before I could go out and do anything. Otherwise, we would get up early, make a mad dash out, and return in time before the nurse came around. Sometimes, I could tell the nurse I would be out for a specific time. I often just wanted to make the nurse's workday easy and smooth. Their day was hard enough.

Andrew had a birthday while I was still in the hospital ward, waiting to go to a rehabilitation centre. Hospital staff were telling me that I was going to rehabilitation the following week, then it was tomorrow. We could not make any grand plans for Andrew's birthday if it turned into a day of travel.

The night before Andrew's birthday, I prepped my sister, Ruth, to buy three pizzas; My brother, Pete, bought the cake, and Andrew and I brought the water. We met in the garden on the hospital grounds with Mum and Ruth's husband, Robert. As we got there, another party was leaving and gave us their balloons. We had a perfect time. It was fun and easy. Ruth was also responsible for bringing plates and cups, but forgot to get some spoons to eat the cake with. To improvise, we tore off the side of the pizza box and used the cardboard as spoons. It was an extraordinary improvisation, and I smile about it now. While everyone ate, I just had a bite here and there.

Andrew ended up having a great party with food, cake, and balloons!

Another time, we met in the garden for a very impromptu McDonald's breakfast. Andrew and I were there with Mum, Esther, my nieces Stephanie and Leeanne, my great-nephew, Kalan, and my great-niece, Aylah. We sat in the sun on Sunday and ate a Macca's breakfast. It was the easiest way to get together with family without dealing with the hospital COVID protocol, and it was also very nice to be in the fresh air and the sun to socialise and have fun.

I was in the hospital ward for around four weeks. It was suggested I go to rehabilitation. Again, no rehabilitation facility wanted me with my needs! I stayed in the hospital a lot longer than was necessary. I needed Andrew to be there so I could be cared for, and it would be easier for everyone. Eventually, with many back-and-forth negotiations, I was finally transferred!

I was also lucky that Catherine, the physiotherapist, worked at the rehabilitation facility.

It was very nice to be at the rehabilitation facility. The food was better, and the environment was calmer. The only problem was that the facility did not have an environment that catered to people with disabilities. I could not fit my wheelchair under the tray tables to eat. The plinths they used for physiotherapy were too narrow, and I feared falling off. The physiotherapy that they had me doing was no different from what I was doing in the ward and what I could be doing at home. After one week at the rehabilitation centre, I went home.

Andrew could manage what I needed to do. With help from support workers that we would hire to help me, and being in my home environment, I could grow stronger and develop my skills as my condition improved.

I was referred to outpatient physiotherapy back at the hospital, but that lasted a week as there was another COVID outbreak and the hospital was locked down.

With all the tips and ideas I received from physiotherapists, I put my routine together to build my strength again.

As well as there being such a significant impact on my physical being, there was also an impact on my hormones and the way the systems in my body functioned.

As a result of all the drugs given to me while I was in a coma, I felt no feelings whatsoever. I did not feel happy or sad. I did not feel love or gratitude. I had no feelings of love for Andrew. The only feelings I had were anxiety. I wondered what was going on. Many times, Andrew came to visit, and Mum would also come. I thought that was fair enough, as she worried as much as Andrew did about me. When Mum saw that I was getting better, she would only visit once a week and let Andrew visit once a week on his own.

On one visit, Andrew and I watched an episode of Taronga Zoo together, and it gave us time to be together, and my connection to him returned. There is a theory that if people listen to the same music, their heart rhythm becomes in sync, so I wonder if watching that program did that for us.

I watched the dating show Love Island on TV late at night and wondered why I had no sexual feelings. It was strange. It was many months later, when I spoke with my psychologist, that he explained that the coma and all the drugs that were given to me suppressed my emotions and that it would take time for me to have the feelings come back. Most of my feelings have come back, but wow, the physiological damage that my body has gone through to save me is mind-boggling.

Not only did the drugs suppress my feelings, but I went

through menopause in the two months that I slept. My skin has become very dry, I suffer from incontinence, and things are just very different.

Waking up after my coma has been like turning pages in a new book. I do not know what is on the next page.

In Pursuit...

- The 'will to live' and get on with life is innate. The human body is strong and will do what it has to to keep living.

- The hospital is where you would think disabilities would be comfortable and accepted, but it does not work. It is like trying to fit a square peg in a round hole.

- Fighting to meet my 'needs' was an ongoing battle. Why did I have to keep fighting for common sense to prevail?

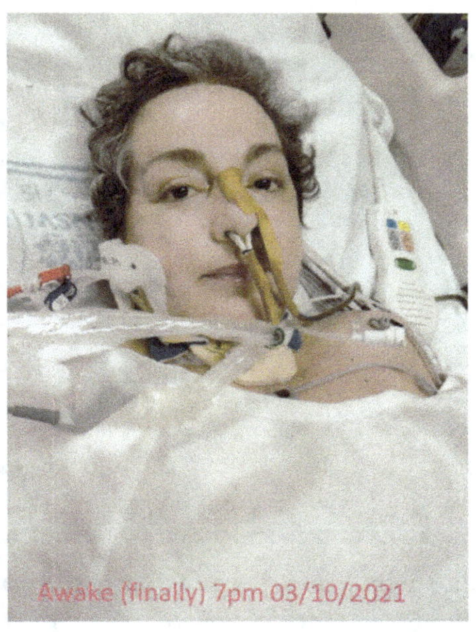

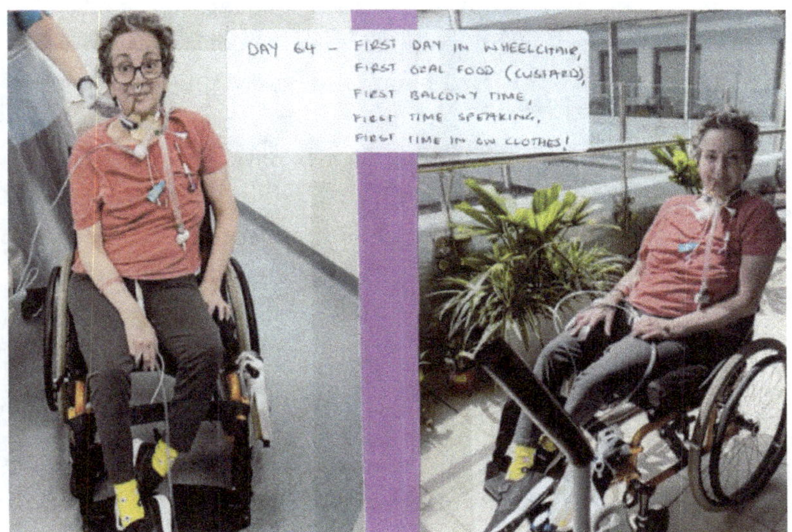

A day of firsts

Chapter 3

At Home

Home is Where the Heart is

Towards the middle of November 2021, two weeks before leaving the hospital, I got two day passes while I was in the ward.

The first time was to visit my dogs where they were boarding.

Andrew and I had planned how to get me in our car. If I got into my power wheelchair in the ward, I could drive straight into our van. Andrew drove us to visit the dogs, and I could steer myself around in my power wheelchair.

Our three dogs are like our children; of course, I wanted to visit them first as I missed them and knew they would have missed me.

Our vet, Camille, has an off-leash park where we could meet on her property. It was a sunny, windy November day. I was wearing a denim jacket to shield me from the cold.

Upon our arrival, the dogs were brought out for our reunion.

As Pupa is a very affectionate, people-pleasing dog, she was more than happy to run and jump up on my lap and give me lots of kisses. Pupa could not get enough of me. Every time Andrew took her off my lap because I was feeling smothered and overwhelmed, she would run and jump back up and start kissing me all over again. Her reaction was a delight, and I loved it. Pupa is eleven years old.

Bronte said a quick hello by jumping on my lap and sniffing. Then, she was busy chasing cars, as usual in the off-leash park. Bronte is a sensitive dog that needs special attention. Bronte is ten years old. Bronte was unhappy that I had left her, and it would take her four months after I got home to trust me again. It was a sad time.

Pixie was the most surprising to see at the off-leash park. She said hello in her unique way, then Andrew put her down, and she was more than happy to follow me as I moved around the park. I found it very adorable to be followed around by Pixie because she hates walking anywhere. She thought I was worth the effort! Pixie is thirteen years old.

At the end of our visit, Camille, our exceptional vet, hugged me and shed some tears. We have a special bond with our vet. She is petite but wears rugged clothes — jeans, a plaid shirt, and boots — daily. Camille is very knowledgeable as a vet and in human life. It was lovely for me to personally thank her for looking after my dogs and for her to see that I was on the mend. She has been our vet for around fifteen years.

Our second ward pass was two weeks after our first. It was a Monday when Mum usually stayed with me in the hospital so Andrew could get jobs done, like getting cars ready for registration.

Andrew had no jobs, so Mum, Andrew, and I went on an adventure. After getting in my power wheelchair and getting in the car, we decided to spend some time at home. On the way home, I asked Andrew to stop at our local Woolworths to buy chicken and bread rolls for lunch.

Arriving home was lovely, and there is nothing like the familiarity of seeing your home. As the front door opened and I drove in, seeing the beautiful paint colour on the walls, my rooms were welcoming and lovely to my heart. I was coming home, ah! Better than a hospital!

Mum suggested I sit out the back while she and Andrew prepared the bread rolls and cups of tea.

I went to pick up the bread roll with avocado and chicken,

but it was too heavy. I was shocked at how weak I was. Andrew had to cut the bread roll in half so I could lift it. A whole bread roll was too heavy!

After lunch, I had a nap. The bread roll took a lot out of me.

I then had this great idea to shower at home in my nice, warm bathroom in my old 'comfortable' wheelchair. Together, Mum and Andrew washed my hair and my body, got me dried and dressed, and let me have another rest in bed. Once they tidied up after my shower, I returned to my power wheelchair and returned to the hospital.

Andrew could not wait for me to return home. He and I were confident we could make it work by employing the right support workers and having family around.

Not being wanted in any ward because of my 'extra' needs and then again having the same issue when we needed to go to rehabilitation made us both question if I would be better going home. Each time, the hospital staff urged us to continue to a ward and then on to rehabilitation. We did what we were told, but in hindsight, I think it would have been easier if I had just come home after ICU and had community nurses come in to dress my heel and neck dressings.

After one hundred and thirteen days in hospital and rehabilitation, I got to go HOME! One hundred and thirteen days is one week off four months. What I was told would be two to three days in the hospital turned into a life-altering event. An operation that has impacted all facets of my life and that I am still recovering from three years on. The disturbing images and thoughts in my mind may never go away, but I know that they are also like waves. At times, it is rough and in your face. At other times, quiet and calm.

Once home, I went about looking for things I could do. One of those things was type. My trusty computer came to my rescue. I was able to use that and my brain to do A LOT! I was able to answer emails and tidy up our invoices and budget.

I follow a heap of YouTube influencers. I started catching

up while I was in hospital on Andrew's laptop, but there was more that I enjoyed watching when I got home.

I also started reading again. Matt, a colleague from an advisory committee, sent me a book to read that was very poignant at the time: The Inside_Track by Peter Sage. It is a very inspirational book about looking 'up' at the possibilities, moon, and stars, and not looking 'down' at your muddy cir-cumstances.

I also frantically started looking for a support worker to help me get ready in the morning, do my exercises, give me breakfast — hot tinned spaghetti — do a bit of housework and cooking, feed me lunch, and then put me back to bed for the afternoon.

I found a great support worker, Nora, during the first week of being home, and she worked very well with me. I discovered that she was very thorough and careful. Nora was from Spain, had a great accent, and was tall, thin, and strong.

Three months after returning home, I wanted to get on the floor, crawl into the shower, and shower like I used to before my hip operation. At the time, I was very shaky on the floor, and I would fall back often, as I still lacked core strength, but I felt that I had to start trying to get back to 'normal.'

I was very saddened when I met new people as they did not know the 'old' me and the potential I had.

Nora was fearful of letting me do things for myself. This made me feel scared, also. I either had to stop trying to take my kind of shower or let Nora go. I chose the latter and kept practising having showers on the floor. In hindsight, I proba-bly tried the shower on the floor a bit too early because I was still so weak, but I felt stronger than when I first got home.

I called myself the five-hour girl, as that was all the time I could stay out of bed before needing to get back into bed and nap.

I had a continuous cough due to having had a tracheotomy. The cough was very inconvenient as COVID was still around, and people who coughed were frowned upon as though they were spreading COVID. I still did not have much of a voice when I got home, and I did not get my voice back for up to a year. I had to be patient and try not to talk so much. It was a perfect opportunity to practise listening more.

My cough became worse when I was tired or had to speak a lot. I felt like I had a lump in my chest, just below my throat, I wanted to cough up and out. The lump also tickled that area and made me cough. It felt strange. I think it was probably bruising from having tubes down my throat. GPs are too busy to answer questions or do not know. Again, I wish I had been given a leaflet about this when I left the hospital.

I contacted my dietitian, Renee, as soon as I got home. I was relieved she knew the old me and was happy to put a plan in place for me to build myself up again. The first thing we did was start taking Sustagen and making sure I was eating enough protein. I was doing well in the eating area. I loved working with Renee, and once I had my eating system in place, I stopped seeing her. About eighteen months later, I noticed that I had not stopped gaining weight and was starting to get on the heavy side. Oh dear! I contacted Renee and told her I was getting fat! She scolded me and told me not to use that word. I tried hard to eat better, but the weight kept increasing, so I took a break from focusing on this.

In addition to nutrition, exercise has been another on-and-off area in my life that I have been working on.

Although I have maintained exercise throughout my recovery, how I did it varied. I took the exercises from the hospital that the physiotherapists had given me. My brother-in-law, John, a physiotherapist, gave me some exercises to add to my collection.

John suggested I put rice into Ziploc bags and lift them as weights, starting at half a kilo. It was a great idea. I can now lift over two kilos with each arm.

One day, I was out and about and heard about Abbey, an

exercise physiologist, on the grapevine through my friend, Kevin. Kevin was telling me how great Abbey was. I finally got Abbey's number and set up an appointment, and she had me standing up, twisting my body, pushing and pulling her around, and doing other great things.

Whenever Abbey came over for my session, I thought she was moving in with her bag, stick, and cushion. Abbey is a little pocket rocket with a very distinct, energetic voice. We laughed a lot together, cried a bit, and worked out that neither of us had the attention span to count to ten.

I asked Abbey to set up an exercise regime, and she did. I am a sucker for punishment and will do all that I can to get fitter and more robust.

Ever since I woke up from my coma, I have been determined to get better. My family and friends put so much effort into keeping me alive that I felt my way of thanking them would be to get better and get on with the rest of my life. It has been challenging, and I have been through some dark times, but I fight back to the surface. I did not think it would take this long and it would be this hard to return to my 'normal.' It feels like I have had an accident, and I am now disabled. People already saw me in a wheelchair, so I am perceived as being better because I am back in my wheelchair, not in a hospital bed.

Sadly, Abbey moved out of my area, so we stopped working together, but I kept doing her prescribed exercises.

While I was working with Abbey, I was experiencing a lot of pain. Abbey suggested I see a physiotherapist.

I got an appointment with Stefan from Innovate Rehab. Stefan was the one I needed at the time. Not only did Stefan work on my physical pain, but he also steered me to work on my pain mindset. A pain mindset is where your brain keeps sending pain signals to body parts no longer injured. You keep feeling pain as a habit or out of fear. I read books and watched Lorimer Moseley's YouTube videos on "pain and the brain."

Slowly, I reduced my pain and became free of it. I had pain for years. It was a lovely feeling to be pain-free. Now and then, I get a 'flare-up' of pain, but I again work through my steps.

Talking about my pain with Stefan helped me to see my pain was wrapped around my fear and trauma and COVID. I had a lot to unpack.

I now see Stefan as an exercise physiologist who is also trained in this area. Stefan can count to ten without losing focus. He likes to play music during our sessions. Anything Crowded House and we will keep getting on like a house on fire! Stefan gave me lots of information on what my muscles and tissues are doing and data on psychology and the body.

I will keep fighting to improve and return to my 'normal.'

I recently started yoga with Andrew. I enjoy that the yoga instructor does a lot of floor work so that I can participate as much as possible. Yoga is another form of exercise I like to do. To have variety, I also do some resistance training and go to the gym to keep my body active.

In Pursuit...

- Healing from the coma is like peeling an onion. Discovering what area needs work, working on it, then finding another area and working on that, and on and on.

- Never give up on becoming the best version of you.

- It is essential to reach out for help to keep the depression at bay.

Chapter 4

Daily Routine after My Coma

My eyes are crusty from sleep as I open them. The crusty flakes fall into my eyes and sting my eyes. The crust is from dried-up tears. Tears that my eyes produce due to sleeping with my eyes slightly open. Tears are made to keep my eyes moist. It is incredible how the body has all these default tendencies to keep it in good shape.

As I roll over from my left side onto my back, blinking my eyes and wiping the dried saliva from the left corner of my mouth, I feel the aches of stiffness from being asleep for hours in one position. As I unfurl my body and move around to ease the aches out of my stiff limbs, my mind starts putting together a to-do list of what I want to accomplish today. What can I do independently, and what do I need help with?

The first thing I need to do independently is sit up in bed and turn my body so my feet touch the carpet. Most days now, I can master this task in one fell swoop. On other days, I struggle as my body may not want to cooperate with my brain; it may take a few attempts, or I ask for some help. On the days when I need help sitting up in bed, I know I will be in for a difficult day, and I need to be patient and kind to myself.

Once I am sitting up, my husband, Andrew, will bring my

wheelchair in from the other room and, rather noisily, lift the footplates with his feet and pull the levers on the inside of each footplate to allow the footplates to swing out onto either side of the back wheel. Once the footplates are out of the way, Andrew brings the chair closer to where I am sitting on the bed. Andrew then opens the bathroom door and manoeuvres around the back of the chair to the front. Andrew positions his body, grabs me under my arms, stands me up, swings me around, and sits me on the edge of my wheelchair. I use my arms to wriggle my bottom back, remembering to bend my torso.

Once in my wheelchair, I swing the right footplate into place, reverse, and wheel into the bathroom. I angle my wheelchair near the toilet. I find the bathroom floor too cold and hard on the soles of my feet, so I have a foam mat that gives me cushioning and warmth. I place my feet on the foam mat, and, using the handrail on the wall beside the toilet, I pull myself up onto my feet. Andrew then pulls my pants down, and I swing around and place my bottom on the cold toilet seat.

We move the wheelchair from in front of the toilet seat so I can swing my legs around to sit more comfortably. I relax my body and let the motions happen, usually accompanied by some bassoon noises. I cut off some toilet paper and yank my left leg up to get the toilet paper in with my hand to wipe myself. I call out, "I'm ready!" and Andrew returns. Sometimes, I must wait as Andrew unglues his eyeballs from his phone. Once Andrew comes back in, I pull myself up into a standing position using the handrail, and Andrew pulls my pants up. Andrew then places the wheelchair behind me, and I sit down, hoping to bend at my waist simultaneously to have a smooth seat. I then use my arms to sit myself back down, swing the left foot plate into place, and push the footplates back down to put my feet on them.

On the way out of the bathroom, I hang a right and pick

up my phone, glasses, and any rubbish I need to put in the bin. I leave the bedroom, turn off the light, and go around the front room of the house, opening the blinds. I go into the kitchen, throw the rubbish out, go to the other side, and turn on the light.

Once I am sitting in my spot at the eating nook, I unload my lap of my glasses and phone. I put my glasses on, open my phone, and see what has been happening while I was sleeping. At the same time, Andrew makes our morning cuppa, gluing and ungluing his eyes from his phone. Once I get my cuppa, I use my mouth to transfer a straw from my water glass to my teacup, and I pretty much drink the tea in ten seconds flat. I love tea!!!

I am now becoming human enough to give Bronte her dog treat for the day. Bronte jumps onto the lounge and I give her a Schmacko strip that I have to break into pieces — otherwise, she tries to swallow the whole strip, which can get messy. Up until Bronte gets her treat, she runs and pounces around the house like a four-year-old puppy. Once she gets her treat, she's an 'old' fourteen-year-old dog who likes to lay around and sleep.

I go back to sit at my nook while Andrew prepares our breakfast. It is winter, so I eat a homemade porridge that Andrew pulverises in batches: a blend of mixed nuts, dates, and oats with a dash of cinnamon. Andrew adds a quarter cup of porridge and half a cup of water, cooks it in the microwave for ninety seconds, and serves it to me with a spoon. It is quite a solid consistency, but I can manage it better, getting it on the spoon and then into my mouth.

After I finish my porridge, I manoeuvre my wheelchair to open the drawer on my left with my right hand. I wish I could use my left hand to open the drawer. It would be a lot more graceful. However, I cannot use my left arm this way as I do not have the necessary control. Not many people know this about me, but my left arm is just a prop. It prevents me from falling to my left and ending up on the floor.

Where was I before I went off on the left-arm tangent? I open the drawer and pull out our tablets and vitamins. As a collective of tablets, we call them 'vitaminka.' It is a word on the back of a packet of savoury snacks not made in Australia. We liked the word so much that we thought we would add it to our everyday life. We also use the word 'medicament' for prescription drugs, and we call grains of rice 'ricelings.'

Andrew puts my vitaminka in a medicine cup and puts it to my lips; like a shot, I put the tablets in my mouth, under my tongue. I take a big sip of water through my straw and swallow, hoping all the tablets go down without hitting my gag reflex and shooting straight out again, water and all.

After this little circus act, I put all the vitaminka and shot glass back in the drawer and pulled out my mocha coffee sachet from the next drawer. The truth is that the engines do not start firing until this coffee is consumed. While Andrew makes my coffee, I ring Mum on the video to say good morning and check in with her.

After I finish my coffee, I like to prepare for the day. I once showed Mum how I do this, and she could not stop laughing. Instead of splashing water on my face, which is impossible to do, I use a spray bottle and spray my hair and face with it. I then wipe my face down with a face cloth, grab my brush, and brush my hair into place. I then apply some moisturiser from a jar I keep in my dresser drawer. Sometimes, the lid hits the floor, and I have to ask Andrew to pick it up; most of the time, the lid stays on the dresser or in the drawer where I can pick it up again.

After I finish doing my hair and face, I brush my teeth. I know what you are thinking: Why not brush my teeth first? I have asked myself that question quite a few times, too. The reason is that my dresser is right inside my bedroom door, so I gravitate there first and, also, after I brush my teeth, I always have to pee.

Brushing my teeth is also a bit of a farcical endeavour. As I manoeuvre my wheelchair past the foot of my bed and veer right at the ensuite door, I push myself up a small ramp and head straight to the sink. My chair can go in under the sink as there are no cupboards. On the right of the sink is a medicine cabinet with everything I need to brush my teeth.

Andrew loads my electric toothbrush with toothpaste the night before and puts it on its stand. I also have a water bottle in the cupboard to rinse my mouth after brushing my teeth.

The process of brushing my teeth is as follows: I first park my wheelchair in the correct position and put the brakes on. I put the face cloth on my lap and open the medicine cabinet door. I pull out my water bottle and place it on the sink. I pull out the toothbrush and turn the tap on to wet the toothpaste on the toothbrush. I then turn the tap off, put the toothbrush on my teeth, and turn the toothbrush on. I brush my front teeth by moving my head around the toothbrush. I then move the toothbrush to the sides and brush there. Teeth brushing is problematic as it requires fine motor skills and, for some reason, my mouth fills with saliva rather quickly. Once I have finished brushing my teeth, I turn the toothbrush off, pull it out of my mouth, pull the toothbrush head off the rest of the toothbrush with the face cloth, and put it in the sink. I then wipe my face with the face cloth and spit out the toothpaste. I put the toothbrush motor back on the stand in the cabinet. I grab the water bottle, take a sip, swish the water around in my mouth, and spit the water and toothpaste out. I rinse my mouth out one more time, and I am done. I now proceed to pack up the rest. I put my water bottle back in the cabinet, rinse the toothbrush, and put it on the shelf. I close the medicine cabinet door. I grab the face cloth and wipe down the sink, place the face cloth on the edge of the sink, and I am done. If it is a good day, my toothbrush will be in the cupboard, not on the floor. If the toothbrush is on the floor, Andrew must pick it up and put it away at some stage in the day.

I then leave the bathroom by turning around one hundred and eighty degrees and going out of the ensuite banking left, leaving down the ramp past my bed and entering the bedroom space.

Now that my teeth are done and my breath has that icy, minty taste, it is time to find my clothes and get dressed for the day.

I need to go into a few rooms to gather my clothes. Most of my clothes are in my walk-in wardrobe. The rest of my clothes are in the formal room on a bedside table that I turned into a hanging rack on wheels.

I have to think about the weather and what I will do that day to decide what to wear. Sometimes, I like to dress nicely when I go shopping. At other times, I just put on jeans and a jumper. When writing this, it is winter, so layers are a must.

I find my underclothes — a bra, a singlet or T-shirt, and a pair of undies. Now for my top layer — a jumper and a pair of jeans or pants. I find all my clothes and call Andrew to help me dress. We take off my jumper and T-shirt that I slept in. Andrew then puts my bra on as I cannot do it up at the back. We then put my T-shirt and jumper on. I then go to pee again and remove my leggings and undies.

After peeing, Andrew helps me put on a clean pair of undies and pants, and as I stand with the handrail in the bathroom, Andrew pulls up my undies, pulls down my T-shirt, and pulls up my pants, tucking in my T-shirt. I hate having my back uncovered in winter.

If I am going out, I need to add shoes, a scarf, and a jacket to my ensemble. Maybe even a beret.

I usually head to my office to do paperwork if I am not going out. I like to tidy up along the way. Put things away in their place, put dishes and cups in the dishwasher, and straighten pillows that Bronte may have messed up. I also like to check that Bronte has enough food and water; if not, I will inform Andrew that a refill is in order.

Once in my office, I turn on the computer, find the to-do list I had probably written the night before, and start working. I always need to add things to my list to do. The additions usually come from my Mum or through emails I must attend to.

Things constantly on my to-do list are writing five hundred words four times a week, finances and budgeting and keeping my spreadsheets in order, banking, exercising, looking after my health and Andrew's health, and making sure I have fun along the way.

At around 11am, I like having tea with one sugar and some oat milk. I might even have a sweet treat like a doughnut, biscuit, or banana for morning tea.

I then return to doing what I must do or go outside and water the plants in 'the oasis' — the outdoor area we have created. The plants have an L-shaped layout on the edge of the back veranda. I think most of the plants are ugly but tend to grow well. The lovely plants I love tend to die slowly or are only annuals. Some of the plants I have just cut back and stuck back into the soil, and they have taken off. I have not figured out how plants work yet. They are a real mystery.

I have enjoyed watching the plants give birth and grow and thrive. I am very joyful for all that nature throws my way in the plant department. I am filled with awe and wonder.

I also love how Bronte lays out in the sun. She knows how to relax and get warm. It is such a peaceful time. Time seems to stand still while this warming is happening. I also like putting my legs in the sun and warming them up. Often, Bronte will get onto my lap, curl up, and sleep — it's such a privilege to be part of that time with her. Unfortunately, I am the one who disrupts our time as I always need to do something else like pee, blow my nose, or get something else done.

I would like to have lunch from around 12.30pm to 1pm. Finding something to eat for lunch is one of the hardest things. It is the most boring meal of the day. I think sandwiches are boring and salads are bland. Everything else takes too much time to prepare or make. We often eat veggie burgers with tomatoes, avocado, and cheese. Or egg on toast. Hot breakfasts for lunch is probably what I enjoy the most. A decadent breakfast throughout breakfast time and lunch may be the way to go.

After lunch, I like to have a coffee and then go to sleep. I can slide off my wheelchair onto the bed without much drama most days. When drama occurs, I usually get stuck between the bed and the wheelchair. I start giggling, and Andrew has to push me onto the bed to be safe. It takes me about an hour to slow down my brain and sleep, and in that hour, I have to pee at least once or twice. Poor Andrew often gets woken up as he has just fallen asleep. He is a very patient man.

Once I get off to sleep, I generally sleep for about sixty to ninety minutes. Before my afternoon nap is part one of the day. I start part two of the day when I wake up from my nap.

Andrew stands me up from my bed and sits me in my wheelchair. We wheel into the bathroom and do the pee routine. Once finished, we have a cup of tea about an hour before dinner.

In the hour, I check my email and see if there is anything I need to attend to. If there is, I will start my computer and do the work. I then have a video chat with the family to see how their day was, and we usually discuss what we are having for dinner. The people I chat with usually include Mum, my sisters, Ruth and Esther, my brother, Peter, and my niece, Leeanne.

Andrew and I then decide what to eat for dinner, heat it, and eat.

After dinner, I will pee again, get on the floor from the toilet, pull up my pants, and start crawling around the kitchen and doing laps. I used to be able to do ten laps around the kitchen in five minutes. After the coma, I started doing one lap, which took about five minutes. Once I felt comfortable doing one lap, I progressed to two laps and did that for a couple of weeks. I then got some more stamina, and I progressed to three laps. I am now able to do three laps in three minutes. I am happy with the progress I am making.

After completing my laps, I crawl towards my bed, kneel in front of it, and launch onto it. Getting onto the bed takes a lot of strength and energy, and I am usually quite tired and out of breath.

My chest is very raspy, and I must cough to sort out the mucus that has built up due to exertion. I work on slowing down my breathing to a normal rhythm. After a few minutes, I feel okay again, and I scoot up the bed and towards my bed-side table. I turn on the television and either watch something on free-to-air or I might watch something on Prime Video. While watching the television, I charge my deep brain stimulation (DBS) device. I must lie down and put the paddle on the battery to let it charge. Charging takes about fifteen to twenty minutes, and I must do it daily. I would much rather have fifteen minutes a day than thirty or so every other day. After charging, I put the charger away and either keep watching television or read something on my Kindle. If I watch a sport, I might do both for a bit.

At 9pm, I will have my tablets, another cup of tea, and a snack. I pee, turn off the television, put away my Kindle, and sleep at 11pm. If I am lucky, I will sleep through the night and wake up at around 7.30am. Often, I wake up through the night because I am sore in my position or need to pee again. The peeing never ends.

In Pursuit...

- Routines help us find our way back to normalcy.

- Each day, I get stronger by finding new ways to go to the bathroom without stressing my body.

- My gravestone plaque will read, "She finally stopped peeing!"

PART 2

LIFE'S HAPPENINGS

Chapter 5
We Are Family

Once upon a time, in the middle of the Mediterranean Sea on a tiny island called Malta, my father, Alfred John Farrugia, the fourth child to Louis and Lucy Farrugia, was born. He was born in Zurrieq, a small fishing village on the southwest coast of Malta, in 1938, just before World War II started. Alfred has five sisters and is the only boy in his family.

Alfred was a handsome, skinny young man with brown eyes and curly brown hair.

My mother, Miriam Spiteri, is the second child born to Paul and Carmen Spiteri. Miriam was born in Santa Venera, smack bang in the middle of Malta, in 1941. Miriam was born in a hospital despite World War II happening all around. Miriam has one brother and three sisters.

Miriam grew into a beautiful young lady with green eyes and wavy brown hair. She had a slim waist and wore a bra padded with tissues to give the illusion of bosoms.

Alfred and Miriam grew up in the same village in Malta, down south in Vittoriosa.

Alfred and Miriam grew up as teenagers in the same street. Miriam's sister and Alfred's sister were best friends. When Alfred romantically noticed Miriam, Miriam is sixteen years old and Alfred is nineteen years old. Miriam worked as a ticket collector for ferries in Malta. Alfred used to pretend to play football near the harbour in Vittoriosa, then get on the last ferry with Miriam. The ferry would then moor in Valletta, and Alfred would walk with Miriam to deliver the tickets and take the day's takings to the ferry office. They would then catch the bus back home to Vittoriosa. On these trips, Alfred romanced Miriam, and they became boyfriend and girlfriend.

When Miriam shares this story with me, I see it like an old black and white movie where Audrey Hepburn plays Miriam and Alfred is played by a young Dean Martin, with soft music playing in the background. Miriam dressed in the latest fashion, sewn by her aunt, with a small, heeled shoe. Alfred wears dress pants and a white button-down shirt with rolled sleeves.

I have heard the story of this courtship hundreds of times and never grow tired of hearing it. I love Alfred's chivalry and Miriam's romantic ways.

I wish their love was smooth sailing all the time, but there were misunderstandings, breakups, getting back together, and everything in between — the realness of all relationships.

They courted for around four years before they were married in 1961.

A year after marriage, Miriam gave birth to Ruth in 1962. Esther was born two years and one day later in 1964. Both pregnancies and deliveries were without any complications.

Ruth and Esther cannot be any more different from one another. Ruth was a tiny baby with fair hair and brown eyes. Esther was a big baby with dark brown hair and brown eyes. Ruth is bossy and quick-tempered. Esther is patient and laid back.

When Ruth was three and Esther was one, Alfred and Miriam immigrated to New Zealand in 1965 and two years later came to call Australia their home. When Miriam applied for her passport, Miriam's name on her birth certificate was Mary Anne.

Alfred and Mary Anne wanted more children. After three miscarriages, Mary Anne was finally pregnant with me. The doctors put a stitch in Mum so I would stay put. When it was considered that I was near full term, Mum had the stitch removed, and three days later, her waters broke. Mum was in labour.

I am the third daughter born to my parents, Alfred and Mary Anne Farrugia.

It was a long labour, over twenty-four hours. The nurse exclaimed to Mum, "You have no idea how to push!" At this stage, Mum was exhausted. I was delivered breach, bottom-first, and I had stopped breathing because of the stress I went through in delivery.

There were no ultrasounds around the time of Mum's pregnancy with me. The obstetrician would feel around the pregnant mother's belly to see how the baby was positioned. While Mum was in labour, further assessment should have been made, and a decision to bring me into the world via caesarean would have prevented me from struggling as I did.

It took the doctors forty minutes to revive and stabilise me. My prognosis was that I had suffered brain damage, but the extent of the effects would not be seen until I grew up. Esther was nearly nine years old when I was born, and Ruth was almost eleven years old.

I was born at Fairfield Hospital in their annexed add-on in 1973. I was christened Martha-Jane Farrugia on the day of my birth in case I passed away. Aunty Polly and Uncle Joe, Mum's aunt and uncle, were my godparents. My name was supposed to be Rebekah. However, my parents did not want to waste a name they liked on a baby girl who may pass away.

But here I am, fifty years on, stuck with the name Martha-Jane for all my life. Maybe my life would have been different had they named me Rebekah. I believe you become the name you are given in life.

I stayed in the neonatal intensive care unit for five weeks after I was born, as I could not suckle. A neighbour in my parents' street suggested to my Mum that she try spoon-feeding me. The next time Mum visited me, she tried this and it worked, so I was allowed to go home.

My parents' response to having a baby that was 'subnormal' was that they would love me like their other two daughters and treat me as though I was 'normal' in the hopes that I would have a good life.

I was a challenging baby to look after, as I cried a lot. My sister, Ruth, wanted to return me from where I came from. Esther wanted to help Mum look after me. I still needed to be spoon-fed, but I also cried a lot, probably from my involuntary movements waking me up. Mum says I never slept through the night until I was about five, probably when I figured out I could lay on my left arm and leg to stop the involuntary movements.

Up until the age of six, Dad used to drive me to the hospital in the middle of the night as I was going blue around my mouth because I was having trouble breathing. Dad would drive me to Randwick Children's Hospital while Mum held me on her lap in the car. It was about a forty-five-minute drive to get there. Dad had a blue Morris that they prayed would not break down. Once at the hospital, I would be given oxygen and stabilised. This trip happened about two to three times a week, and Dad would get up the following day, get ready, and go to work. He never complained.

At age six, portable home nebulisers were made available and Mum could give me oxygen and medicine at home in the middle of the night. When I lay down, my lungs fill with fluid, and this makes it hard for me to breathe.

At the age of nine months, I started talking. My first word was 'Esther,' calling out to my sister with whom I shared a bedroom and who was my best friend. My parents saw in my eyes that I could understand, so they never baby-talked to me.

I had trouble holding onto objects when they were given to me. My parents learned that they had to wait for me to close my hand or put their hand around mine to close my hand. I still have trouble with it, and I still need help with it — all part of my cerebral palsy. I was diagnosed as having athetoid cerebral palsy at the age of three.

Mum started looking after children to inspire me to learn from them. I did not begin sitting up independently until I was eighteen months old. Mum taught me how to sit up by placing pillows around me and behind my back and taking them away slowly. It took a while for my core to become strong enough to manage the involuntary movements. I also tended to fall to the left side, so I had to learn to put my left hand on the ground to hold me up and have my left leg bent and under my right leg to keep my left side from involuntary movement.

I never crawled on my hands and knees as my knees had no padding on them, and the knee bone on the floor hurt a lot, so I crawled around on my bottom using my hands to lift myself from the floor enough to swing myself forward.

Mum was revolutionary in the way she looked after me. Mum always reminded me to swallow, so I did not dribble, and to sit up straight, as my body likes to lean to the left. Mum never accepted my dribbling and sitting crooked. Thanks to Mum, I do not dribble much and sit relatively straight.

Mum started taking me to physiotherapy at age three. My Mum's journey consisted of pushing me in my pram, walking to the train, catching a train to Parramatta, catching a bus to North Parramatta, and then walking to Northcote to take me to my physiotherapy session. It was a full day of travel that happened twice a week. Mum did everything she could to look after me instinctively and with professional recommendations.

Emotionally, I was attached to Mum, and some of my early school reports have written in them that, 'Martha is too attached to her mother.' As a fifty-year-old, I am still attached to my mother, and so are my sisters and my brother, who was born after me. It is the way our family is. We go out and do our own thing, and when we are done, we return to Mum.

The relationship with my Dad was, of course, different but still good. Dad always loved me and accepted me. He was incredibly wise. If I were struggling physically, he would say things that would help me change my perspective or understand why life was more challenging but still attainable. Dad would say, "Even though it takes you twice as long to do things, you never give up."

When I was eighteen months old, Dad went to Malta and saw that my younger cousin was walking. Upon returning to Australia, Dad tried to stand me against the kitchen cupboard and encouraged me to walk to him. I would slip down the side of the cupboard. Walking never happened.

Dad would take me to McDonald's, carry me in, sit me on a seat, order our burgers, and then patiently feed me. I have always loved the way my Dad fed me. He would give me small bites and never rushed me. My brother, Peter, feeds me the same way Dad does. Pete also feeds his daughter the same way.

Dad would bring home electronic games for me to play with. Our first Nintendo handheld game featured Mickey Mouse catching chicken eggs. The whole family played the game, and Mum clocked it! The game went from a score of nine hundred and ninety-nine back to zero.

Dad then brought home a video game that we plugged into the TV. We played Alien Invaders and Pac-Man on it. Dad bought the game for me, but Mum and Ruth took over playing it.

Then, Dad decided I needed a computer, so he brought one home and had me direct him to set it up. The thing was useless, so I sold it and bought a real computer, printer, and desk. Dad set up the flat pack desk as I explained how to do it. We then did the same with the computer. It worked! Dad and I worked well together; I was the brains and he was the brawn.

Dad always encouraged me to do all the hard things I wanted. When I was twenty-five, I wanted to learn how to drive, so once a week Dad would drive me to a specialised driving school forty-five minutes away from home and sit and wait for me to take my lesson, then drive me back home. Driving, for me, was hard work. Trying to control my body and have it do what I wanted at the right time was a lot. In the middle of winter, with the air conditioning in the car at top speed, I would be in a T-shirt and sweat so much that I could wring out my shirt after just an hour of driving.

For one of my lessons, I drove back home on the motorway. While on the motorway, my instructor, Keith, was concerned about a truck with a crooked load in front of us. Keith asked me to overtake the truck so he could signal for them to pull over. We pulled the truck over, and then Keith got out and spoke with the driver. Keith got back in the car, and I got back into the stream of traffic and drove home to say "Hi" to Mum, and then we went back to the driving school.

I persisted and took my driving test, which I failed. I stopped taking lessons as it was getting too expensive, and driving was too hard, but at least I tried.

Dad encouraged me in my pursuit of having children. I did not know until after he passed away how much he cried when my IVF cycles failed.

Dad and Mum were always brave for me. They put on a brave face, supported me, and cried behind my back.

My relationship with my eldest sister, Ruth, was okay. Ruth was the top dog in the house and did not want to hang out or have too much to do with me. She was bossy and scary. We bonded over food, as she was happy to feed me at parties. Ruth's first husband, Mark, was kind to me. As a seven-year-old, he would buy me Smurfs from the petrol station and let me raid his Navy bag for loose change. Ruth would go through the bag before me and take out his undies. Ruth and I share a love for cricket and seventies music.

In my twenties, I would go to Ruth's one night a week and babysit her children so she and her husband, Robert, could go out.

My relationship with my sister, Esther, was very different. Esther would take me out shopping and to events. Esther even took me as her bodyguard to break up with one of her boyfriends. Esther always looked after me and shared her things with me. When Mum went to Malta with Peter in the eighties, Esther was my 'Mummy.' One day, I learned a valuable lesson from Esther. I had to do my homework before going out to play after school. On this particular day, I got home from school and went out to play. After dinner, I was too tired to do my homework. Esther exclaimed, "You should have done your homework before going out to play." From that day on, I always did my homework or work before playing.

When Esther had her two daughters, Stephanie and Emily, she let me be a big part of their lives. I babysat and, at other times, they slept over at my place. Andrew and I also helped with homework and assignments. We all had fun together.

Stephanie's middle name is Jane. She was given my middle name to be strong and determined like me.

My brother, Peter, was born in 1981. My mother was distraught at the thought that she could have a difficult labour again, so she asked the obstetrician to deliver Peter via caesarean. Peter was born perfectly healthy.

I always wanted a baby brother as I did not want to be the youngest child in the family. I did not want to be spoiled. Peter was born eight years after me and was my real dolly. I got to name him Peter, after a doll Ruth had. One day, I pushed him backwards and forwards in his pram so he could sleep. The pram was going off track, so I popped a wheelie to fix it and fell off my chair; the pram tipped back, and Peter fell out the back of the pram onto my lap. So, I dropped him...on his head!

Peter, or Pete, as we affectionately call him, was always angry at me for naming him Peter. He exclaimed, "Why couldn't you have named me John, John Rambo!" He loved watching John Rambo and playing armies. Pete and I grew up as friendly siblings. However, he would always run past me and give me big horsey slaps on my thigh. He would always leave a nice red handprint on my leg. Mum would tell me not to react so Pete would not get into trouble with Dad.

Pete has fair hair and blue eyes. He is easy-going but impatient.

Peter was hyperactive as a child, and since Mum and Dad had not had an active baby for seventeen years, it was a real shock. Pete was a climber. He climbed onto the fridge, the glass fish tank, and the roof of the house. He loved to climb.

Pete now has a daughter, Amelia, who is a climber; we love watching her be like Pete. Pete is quite surprised at what she gets up to, but we are nonplussed. We are ready for what Amelia has in store for Pete because we went through it with him.

Amelia's middle name is also Jane. Her parents wanted her to be named after someone strong, resilient, and inspiring, a fighter who never gives up. And she is determined and intelligent, just like her aunty!

Leeanne is Ruth's eldest child. She is two years younger than Pete. Leeanne spent much of her childhood at our place with Dad, Mum, Pete, and I. As the first grandchild, she was precious to Mum and Dad. Leeanne and I shared a room whenever she was over. We have always got on well. Leeanne is ten years younger than me.

When Leeanne was four years old, I started taking her shopping with me. Leeanne would push me around in my wheelchair, peeking around the side to see where she was going, as she was not tall enough to see over my head. We loved going shopping together. We would look at the toys she wanted to see and then at the clothes and music I wanted to look at. We would have KFC for lunch. I would order a burger, Leeanne would order chicken nuggets and chips, and we would share a Fanta. More often than not, Leeanne would knock over the can of Fanta and we would have to clean it up.

Every time this happened, I would tell Leeanne, "Lucky, this didn't happen with your Mum, or she would be yelling at you right now!"

I think I brainwashed Leeanne into liking green, as green is also her favourite colour. Leeanne is the odd girl in our family, with blonde hair. When Leeanne was twenty-one, she dyed her hair brown, and we were devastated. She was our blonde girl. Leeanne dyed her hair back to blonde soon after and never did that again.

Leeanne is married now and has two children, a boy and a girl. When the children were younger, they would come over for craft days and we always had lots of fun together.

My nephew Rhys and I always get on well. We have always respected each other and got up to some crazy stuff. There was a time when Rhys would ride over from his house to mine, as we lived in the same suburb, and make me lunch. Rhys is a real homebody like his Dad, so he rarely went out with me.

Rhys is married and has a young boy and a young girl. Rhys' son is a social butterfly; we have fun and laugh together.

All the children in my family are okay with me being in a wheelchair and are happy to help me when I need help.

In Pursuit...

- Family makes you who you are. By believing in me, they gave me a solid foundation to give life a good go. I was given responsibility, I was accepted for my limitations, and, above all, I was loved.

Mum and Dad

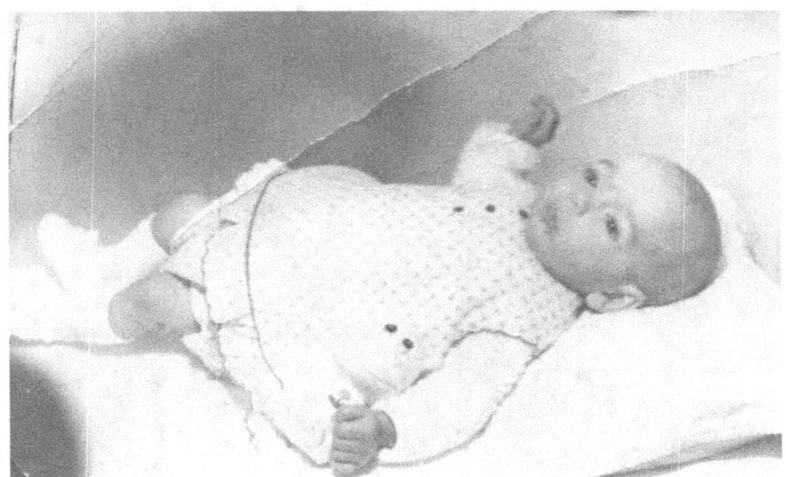

Me with my head shaved, aged six months old

Me in my prams

In the spastic pram

Me on my bikes

Esther, Dad, Ruth, Mum, Pete in Mum's tummy,
and me at Ruth's wedding

Peter, Esther, Ruth, and me

Learning to drive

Chapter 6
Education and Work

Education has always been important in my life. As far back as I can remember, I have always had a book, paper, pencils, or typewriter/computer in my vicinity.

I did not feel like I had 'moved' into our house with Andrew until my computer arrived, was set up, and I was using it.

I started my education at three and a half years old. I went to a special school for crippled children. Back in the seventies and eighties, that was considered an okay name for a school. Now, it would be frowned upon. I still like the 'special' part, though. I felt special at that school. It was pretty progressive in helping feed my mind academically as well as helping me learn how to manage my disability so that I could do personal care tasks on my own.

I started preschool at the cottage. You had to go down a steep concrete hill to get to it. As I was small, wheelchairs were too big at the time. I used a 'Charley Kart' — Charley Karts were very low to the ground. My legs were out straight in front of me. I had a wheel under each arm the size of dinner plates, and there was a small castor behind my bottom at the back and one at the front under my feet. They were an excellent way to get around as infants. The Charley Karts had no brakes, so I had to go down the path slowly.

I got my first small wheelchair when I was about six years

old. I had one at school and one at home. It was great to finally have a wheelchair at home; otherwise, Dad had to carry me around, or I had to sit in a pram. Mum got me a big pram for disabled children, and I refused to sit in it. That pram was not for 'normal' children.

I remember watching Play School every morning at pre-school, and I was hungry to learn. Every class had a teacher and a teacher's aide. The school had a big tree, and underneath that was a fishpond with fish. It was very cool.

I do not remember much about the first couple of years. In year three, I was introduced to using an electric typewriter and my whole world opened up even further as I could type a lot faster and easier than I wrote and keep up a bit better with the pace of my brain.

At around primary school age, we were taken to the shops where we learned to pass over money and collect our change. We also went around the shops and looked at what we wanted to see. In the sports area, games were adapted; wheelchair cricket and wheelchair football were what we played at school.

In year four, I had a great teacher, Mrs Webb, who saw my potential to be 'integrated' into a 'normal' school, public school. The process started in year four, but I did not attend public school until midway through year five. The reasons were that there were no public schools with ramps. One school near my area got ramps put into two classrooms and the library, and I could go. I was put into a composite class year four/five/six. I flourished. I came first in my class that year. The girl I beat was annoyed and said, "If you hadn't come to this school, I would have come first."

I had the same teacher at primary school in years five and six. He was a great teacher who was able to support me well with my disability and still challenge my mind.

As I was approaching year seven, I was worried that I would be put in the dummies' class because I was in a wheel-chair. I remember pleading with my year six teacher, saying,

"They're not going to put me in the dummies' class, are they, sir?" He assured me they would not.

I had to go to a different school than all my peers. The school they all went to had lots of stairs. It was the same high school that my sisters went to. I felt sad that I could not follow in their footsteps and go to that school. Instead, I went to a school in another area. A new high school had been built with ramps.

I was put in the second-highest class of my year and stayed there throughout high school. If my class was in a demountable building, I would be transferred to the highest class. The teachers respected my work ethic and my diligence.

The wheelchair I had when I started year seven had a tray built in underneath to hold my books and bag. My electric typewriter hung in a bag on the back of my chair. It was cumbersome to get from class to class, have my typewriter pulled out, pull out my textbook and paper, set up, do my lesson, pack up, and go to the next class and do it all again. We had seven lessons per day. I then had to go home and do my homework.

In year seven, I had this great maths teacher, Miss Esson, who also looked after my needs as a student with a disability. Miss Esson asked the Rotary Club to fund a scooter for me to get around to my classes. It was a great help. The chair rotated so I could line up to the side of the desk, spin around, and be sitting behind the desk.

Miss Esson also rallied for me to have a standing frame that I used to stand up in art and science classes.

I made friends in all my classes, and they were happy to help. I kept up in all my classes.

Dad helped me with the fine motor skills of drawing with a compass and protractor for maths homework. I had to tell Dad everything that he had to do. He was my hands, and I was the brain. My parents never helped me with my homework, as they were taught differently. I always did okay.

In year eleven, everything unravelled. The school added one more lesson to the day, so we had one more set up and pack up. All my teachers changed through the first half of the year. Too much content was being taught, as well as too much homework and too many assignments. I could not keep up. I would take days off to catch up, then scurry like a rat on a wheel trying to keep up again. And the pressure to study hard was just too much. I spoke to my mentor about leaving, and he said 'no.' After my seventeenth birthday, I had enough. Dad was in Malta, and I convinced my Mum to let me quit. I felt like a failure that I could not complete my HSC, Higher School Certificate. But it was all too much. I learned later that my subjects could have been split, and I could have worked on a lesser workload to completion. If only they had presented that option to me earlier.

After dropping out of school, I stayed home, gathered my energy, strength, and determination for a few months, and set off on my next educational adventure.

I studied a few introductory courses. The following year, we went to Malta.

When we returned from Malta, I was determined to further my education, as I was annoyed that I had not completed my HSC. I discovered I could do the HSC equivalent at TAFE, Technical and Further Education College, called TPC, Tertiary Preparation Certificate. I did the one-year course over two years. Instead of doing six subjects over a year, I did three subjects in one year and three in the following year. It was perfect for me. Each lesson ran for two hours and, often, the next teacher came into our classroom, so I did not have to move rooms.

I did well in TPC and got accepted into both TAFE and university to do accounting. I chose university. I started studying full-time at the university, and it was way too much work. When I started university, I was still coming to terms with the suicide of two of my cousins. Somehow, my brain shut down when they died, and I could not take in or process as much information. I ended up taking a semester off and trying to find work.

Work was something I had no idea how to do. Computers were still new and not used much in workplaces. I could not use my hands to write things down, and a lot of workplaces were not wheelchair accessible. I went to the CES, Commonwealth Employment Service, and asked for help to find a job. The lovely lady gave me a number to contact an employment agency specialising in finding employment for people with disabilities. The employment consultant tried her best, but it was heartbreaking. I was happy to try anything. The employment consultant found me an internship with Blacktown City Council, which was looking to hire someone with a disability. I went to the interview; I was then sent for a medical, which I passed. I then got a letter saying I did not have the right qualifications for the job. I was heartbroken. The truth was that the council did not have the proper set-up to have me work for them. The council could not manage my inability to write on paper. The job I went for required me to write in a ledger — I am pretty sure that now it is all done on computers. The council wanted to hire someone with a medical disability, not a physical disability, to tick their box. An internship does not need any qualifications, just literacy and numeracy.

I then asked the employment consultant to put me in a sheltered workshop environment to work in data entry with other people who had cerebral palsy. I just wanted work experience. I had a lot to learn about work. I had never been in a work environment before. I was twenty-three years old. I did not know how to fill in a timesheet, how to fill in a sick leave form, or how to apply for holidays. It was all new to me.

The data entry was easy to do, and I was given other assignments from another division, and I enjoyed that. A lot of the other workers had less disability than me but were happy to be in this sheltered place, and I guess, looking back now, I can see why. The workers with disabilities were a lot older and subjected to the culture of their time. It was only in my twenties and thirties that mainstream work opportunities became available. I did not stay working at Centre Data for very long as the organisation that owned Centre Data, The Spastic Centre, wanted to 'own' me and take control of my life. No, thank you! I am my own person, and I make my own decisions.

I decided to go back to university and try to finish my degree by taking two subjects at a time. It was a good thing I went back to university because it was then that I met Andrew!

I had the opportunity to become employed by the university and enjoyed working there. At the end of the year, my work ended.

Studying at university was hard as I was not given the support I needed, which were scribes. When I did have scribes, I did well, but when I did not, I felt unsupported. I also discovered that I did not like accounting. I changed my major to information systems. But again, the proper support was not in place, so I felt frustrated.

I applied to TAFE for an advanced web site design and management diploma. I was determined to work, so I sent my resume to around forty website design businesses. Two places rang and invited me for interviews. As part of the phone call, I would ask, "Are there stairs in your building?" The reply was always, "Yes, we can't cater for a wheelchair." The interview was rescinded. I was crushed. I felt like someone with all this potential but no way to use it. I could not get into buildings, and I could not use my hands to write. I felt hopeless.

On the day the interviews were rescinded, I received a letter from TAFE accepting me into the website course. I had all the support I needed and got distinctions in all my subjects.

The physical disability liaison officer offered me employment, to teach one-on-one website subjects. I loved the challenge.

While working at TAFE, I also completed a certificate four in workplace assessment and training. It was a brutal certificate I had to do on a Saturday.

I worked at TAFE for three terms before taking a break.

I found an opportunity to volunteer at Fusion. At first, the staff, who were also volunteers, did not quite know what to do with me. Slowly, I was given tasks that I would complete, and they learned that I was dependable. At a point, I had to step in and tell the team leader not to decide what I could and could not do but to ask me to do something, and I would figure out how to get it done.

I ended up working for the team leader, organising his diary. I also started an internship. It was a lot of work to work and study.

I did many jobs at Fusion and learned a lot about my capabilities. I managed the diary for the team leader and worked on significant research projects.

I was asked to do a certificate three in youth and community services. After completing the course, I was asked to run the training program. The assignments were pulled from many areas of the training program. I gathered them all together into a booklet. The booklet was used to give the students all their assignments the semester after I left.

After I ran training for six months, I decided to do an advanced diploma in counselling and family therapy that my counsellor had done. The course took two years to complete and was run differently. There was a three-day teaching component and then a ten-week assignment component. There were also meet-ups with other students to do work together. It was a good balance, and I was able to make it work for me.

All these jobs showed me my intellectual and physical worth because I found my way to get things done creatively and to completion.

I got tired of working so hard in the volunteering space and not being paid that I decided to look for a paid job.

My sister and a church friend were both working for NOVA. I was intrigued to see if they could help me get a job. I set up a meeting with NOVA's CEO. The meeting happened, and instead of asking for help finding a job, I wondered if I could work at NOVA. The CEO asked me to start work as a job coach the following Monday. Training would be on the job. I said, "Yes!" I arrived at my job on Monday and just learned as I went. After two or three days, I was left to teach as I saw fit. I was unhappy with the training material, so I created my own. The job coaching material I made was then delivered through-out NOVA's offices. I enjoyed training people to look for work and supporting where they were. My heart went out to some of the circumstances faced by the people looking for work, and I always made the job club a safe place. After a couple of weeks, the participants would come in with smiles instead of frowns.

I wanted the job club participants to feel good about them-selves despite unemployment. I had a morning class of new trainees and an afternoon class of active job seekers, which was quieter.

Also, while working, I completed my certificate four in coaching, specialising in the cycle of life. After completing my counselling and family therapy study and practising for a bit, I noticed that I did not want to work on the past with clients; instead, I wanted to work on their goals and how to move for-ward. I wanted to work with people to pursue their dreams. It is great to untangle the past to have a clear path forward, but how do you pave the way to move forward towards your dreams? It excites me to dream and then make that dream a reality.

I worked at NOVA for about four years and needed a break.

While at NOVA, some people from my high school year organised a high school reunion. I was NOT going. I watched the conversation on Facebook, and about an hour before the reunion started, I said to Andrew, "We ARE going!" I am thrilled I went. Everyone was friendly and funny and lovely. The clique were still the clique. Everyone agreed that high school was socially stressful.

I wanted to apologise to one guy, Adam. His Mum was my teacher's aide and would stand me up in his science class. I shared that I was sorry if he was embarrassed that his Mum always came into his science class. He said, "No, I wasn't embarrassed. It was nice to see my Mum happy at work." I was glad I got to clear it up.

I heard about a Living My Way support coordinator and plan manager role. I loved the philosophy behind how Living My Way came to be. I was encouraged to apply for the role, and so I did.

The interview had an extraordinary question in it that I feel God helped me answer. The question was about what you do once you have read the information on a new member. The answer I gave was, "I would ring the member and ask them to tell their story in their own words. Not to assume that the information given is always correct." I think this answer got me the job. I loved my job at Living My Way. I loved chatting with the members and supporting them in their journey. I loved fighting for and with them in the NDIS, National Disability Insurance Scheme, space. I loved helping make life and wishes more possible, valuable, and comfortable.

The tricky thing about the role was that it took a lot of energy out of me, both physically and mentally. There came a time when I had my battle in the NDIS space as well as what I was doing for my members. It all got too much, and I burnt out. I needed to leave after eighteen months. I still miss that role. The culmination of all my studies and life experience made me a perfect fit for that role.

I took a year off to recover and sort out my own NDIS issues.

I missed my role at Living My Way. I loved what I could contribute to people with disabilities: hope and knowing they were not alone on their NDIS journey. I also felt that I role-modelled determination, showed others what was possible if they put their mind to it and kept trying.

In 2016, I attended the one hundred and fifty year celebration dinner for my primary school. It was an adorable night. The people who attended were from my year. They were the friends I have always had in my life since primary school. The reunion shared that a family of four generations had attended the school because the school was small and family oriented.

I am grateful for all the work experience and outstanding achievements I made while working at Fusion, NOVA, and Living My Way.

After my hip surgery, I studied professional styling as part of my recovery. I have always been interested in fashion but thought it was not very sensible. Being given a second chance at life, I thought it was time to follow my heart and study something I was interested in and passionate about. Fashion is a complex area to learn. It is not a strength of mine, but I love it all the same.

In Pursuit...

- I was academically driven as that was the only part of my life where I could compete evenly.

- I have had to go through a side door to gain employment as I do not feel it is fair to compete with non-disabled people for employment.

Preschool —at the special school

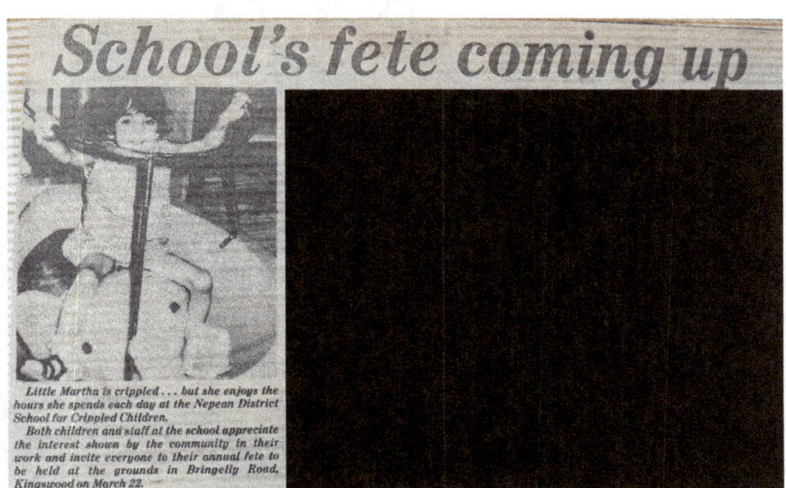

A newspaper article

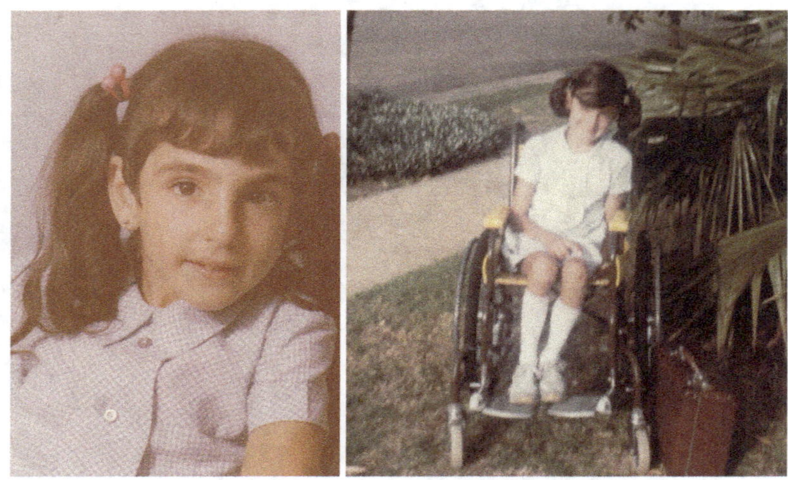

Primary school at the special school

Year ten at high school

Chapter 7

Boys, Boys, Boys, and other Friendships

I have not been seen any differently than how I was seen as a baby, a child, an adolescent, and an adult woman. As much as people are said to be taught socially how to treat people with disabilities, I think we all have a primal instinct and reaction in the way we first see people and interact with them. I do it, too. I am no different to anyone else.

Reactions that I have experienced include thinking I am stupid, being seen as less than, being seen as more than, being seen as fragile, being ignored, and being put on a pedestal.

We all want to be given a fair go. I want people to take me at face value, say "Hi" and take it from there.

It is something I am still working on doing myself, stripping back the body armour I have up in case of an uncomfortable reaction.

Let us begin from the beginning. Mum was a socially clever lady who came up with the idea of looking after children younger and older than me so I could learn to copy them physically. To learn to sit up and crawl and play. Along with encouragement and physical help from my Mum, I wanted to play with the other children, so I eventually developed physically.

In year four at special school, a boy named Mark Philips was in my class. Mark had dark blond hair and brown eyes. He was quiet and gentle. He became my boyfriend. At that age, you say you are boyfriend and girlfriend and hang out. We never kissed or anything because we had obstacles: our wheelchairs. I dropped Mark in year five because I was leaving my special school.

I saw Mark from time to time growing up. I saw him at our local shopping centre. We always stopped and chatted to each other. Mark passed away when we were twenty-one. He had a muscular degenerative disease that killed him. He will always be the kindest boy I have ever known.

I grew up playing with children in my neighbourhood. One particular boy I was good friends with, Michael, was a rugged boy with fair hair. Michael liked to build things. I often went to his place because he had a massive Lego collection. Michael would come over and collect me. He was unafraid of pulling my wheelchair up the stairs at the back of his house. We would play Lego all morning, and then his stepmum, Sandra, would call us for lunch. We would eat Sao biscuits with cheese and tomato and drink orange cordial. I loved going over and feeling like any other kid. Michael had a cubby house in the garage roof that I could climb into because each step up had a landing. It was so cool to be able to get up into the cubby.

Michael and I used to put the tent up in the front yard of his house and my backyard. At my place, I would take a pillow and have lots of stationery around to write down my thoughts or draw.

The most memorable thing Michael did for me was attach my wheelchair to his bike, and we would zoom around the streets. Michael was strong and loved making things happen. I would go fast, and I had so much fun. We got good at me being towed behind Michael and leaning into the corners. I loved the speed and the ease. Until one day, we were going fast on the road, and I leaned the wrong way. My wheelchair tipped over sideways. My knees, elbow, and shoulder kissed the gravel. Michael ran to get Mum. Mum picked me up, took me home, and cleaned up my wounds. It took a while for my knees to heal. Mum was not angry at me as she knew what we were doing and knew it was a way for me to have fun. I am proud of those scars, reminding me of an adrenalin-filled time. We never rode like that again.

I was friends with Banu, who lived next door to us. I would park my wheelchair at the bottom of the stairs, crawl up, and knock on the door. Banu and I played with dolls, stationery, and clothes and talked about life.

The girls in the two houses at the end of the cul-de-sac were scared of me. Narelle and Megan would never let me go over and play. Mum would get angry at their fear of my disability and tell me that I did not need girls like that in my life. I loved that Mum did not confront their parents.

Just before I started primary school, Mum took me to pick up materials for my school uniform. I met a girl named Susan, who was a year behind me. Susan became my best friend when I was in year six. We are still good friends now, forty years later. Susan is fair-haired and has blue eyes and fair skin. Dad often drove me over to spend the day with Susan during primary and high school. Susan lived on a chicken farm. Susan's Dad would put the wheelchair on the tray of his ute and I would sit in my chair; Susan would stand beside me, and her Dad would take us paddock bashing around the property. Oh, the adrenaline. I would be smiling from ear to ear.

When I started primary school, my best friend was Michelle. I met Michelle in the library. Michelle was tiny, and I thought she was in year four, but she was in year six. I sat with the sixth graders when I was in year five. Because my special school had prepared me so well by teaching me advanced maths, I could give Michelle her year six maths answers, even though I was in year five. It meant a lot for me to make friends easily in primary school, and I did.

When I first went to primary school in the middle of year five, Jeremy started teasing me immediately. The reason why he teased me was that there was another girl in the class who had a disability that he teased. I could not say Jeremy's name, so I called him Germany. Jeremy soon learned that even though I also had a disability, the other girl and I were different people. Jeremy and I became friends, and I sometimes played marbles with him and his friends. Jeremy started calling me 'chicken legs' because my legs were thin, but it was all good fun.

My first crush was in year six. His name was Damian. Damian had his hair parted in the middle and flicked back, brown hair, brown eyes, and olive skin. Damian shared a desk with Cameron near the back of the class. Damien talked too much, so he had to come and share my desk and sit next to me. Whenever his punishment was over, I would tell him to behave so I could have the whole desk to myself. Sure enough, he would return to my desk within a few days. Damian did not complain about sitting at my desk. We got on well. I even got invited to his birthday party.

I had many crushes in high school, but I do not think the guys ever knew.

There were two guys I hung out with, Kevin and Michael, but we were always just friends. My friends Jennie, Michael and Kevin, would all come over, and Mum and Dad would cook us lunch.

Kevin was tall and had blond hair and green eyes. He was a gentle giant. Michael had brown hair and eyes. He was tall and thin. Michael's Mum and grandparents were friendly and very accepting of me.

Jennie was my friend from year seven to year ten. She would help set up my typewriter and then pack it up again at the end of the lesson. Jennie had fiery red hair and blue eyes. We were always laughing about something. Recently, Jennie and I started meeting again fortnightly for catchups. I was fortunate that I made friends quickly and that they helped me. They even pushed me around from class to class when I was in my manual wheelchair.

There was one boy in my class who hated me. He called me 'spastic' regularly. He hated me because I always did better than he did in exams and assignments. Even though bullying today is a no-no, I am glad I was bullied, as it made me stronger.

High school was gruelling and I have always said that if I could survive high school, I could survive anything.

While in high school, I made friends with a girl named Lisa. Lisa was a year or two older than me. She had brown hair and eyes. Lisa took me to the local neighbourhood centre after school. There was a guy, Craig, who used to attend. Craig was a bad boy, but I had a crush on him. Craig looked and acted like James Dean. He found out I liked him, so I ignored him because I was embarrassed. I went on an outing to Wonderland with the neighbourhood centre and Craig went too.

Because I was ignoring Craig, he decided to come and carry me off one of the rides I had just finished riding on. I could not ignore him anymore while I was in his arms. Craig sat me in my chair and told me he liked me as a friend, was a bad boy, and was not good for me. After that, everything was good, and we became friends.

Valentine's Day was always awkward in high school. One year, I received yellow roses from my friend Michael. He made sure I knew that yellow roses represented 'friendship.' He wanted me to receive flowers on Valentine's Day. Sweet!

A year or so after I left high school, Mum and Dad took Pete and me to Malta to live. I spent much time in Malta with my cousin, Christian, and his girlfriend, now his wife, Stefania. Christian is a big brute with dark brown hair and brown eyes. Christian is intelligent and did not have to study much to come close to the top in his engineering classes at university.

Stefania has light brown curly hair and brown eyes. She is

of a slight build and is academic. We went out a lot together, and Stefania was very gracious. Stefania would let me sit in the front seat, and she would sit in the back seat along with my wheelchair.

I also went out with my Aunty Gemma to athletics days at the local sports ground in Marsa.

Malta hosted the Small Nations Games in 1993.

When we got to Malta very early on, Mum, Pete, and I went with Aunty Gemma, Mum's sister, to watch my cousin, Sue, compete in an athletics competition. Because Malta is not a big country, you can get up close and personal with just about anyone. We cheered on all the competitions that were taking place and chatted with the competitors as they went by.

The hundred metres for men took place, and we congratulated the winner. The winner locked eyes with me. He kept chatting with everyone while only looking at me. His name was Mario, and my Aunty knew him. A friend of my cousin's noticed the eye-locking thing and commented to me, so it was not just my imagination!!!

Mario has dark brown hair, tanned skin, beautiful blue eyes, and a massive smile!!!

A day later, when I talked to my cousin, Christian, I told him I had met Mario. My cousin exclaimed, "I know him!"

I replied, "Well, next time you see him, give him my phone number!" It was so exciting. Christian met up with Mario and gave him my phone number, and about a week later, Mario rang me, and we chatted for about one hour. I was in lurve and I had a crush. Mario asked me out, and I thought I would have my first boyfriend. Mario picked me up, and Mum gave her usual masterclass on how to fold and pick up a wheelchair to put it in the boot and the reverse, leaving Mario with, "If you get stuck, ask Martha, and have a good night." So there I was in the car with Mario driving...to go pick up his girlfriend, Isabelle...OMG! I was devastated, and everything else. But I played it cool. Isabelle was lovely, and we went out and had a great time. I met many other athletes who were all funny and friendly.

When Mario took me home, Mum was sleeping, so he was happy to take my wheelchair upstairs. I could get myself up the stairs then, so it was all good. After Mario left, I went and let Mum know I was home, and she was surprised I was upstairs and disappointed she did not hear us bring the chair up. It was 1.30am, so I understood that she would be asleep.

The next day, I told my family what happened while picking up the girlfriend on the way, and everyone was disappointed; there was no island holiday romance for me.

Mario still rang, and we still chatted. I went to athletic meets and went out with Mario and his girlfriend. Mario and all of the athletics group took me out for my twentieth birthday. They all put in and bought me a Swatch watch. My birthday was in a garden restaurant in the evening, and it was a warm night. It is very different to my winter birthdays in Australia. I loved it.

When I met Mario, he was studying architecture at university. Mario told me he had been taught not to add ramps in case it would ruin the design's aesthetic. He was now questioning this teaching as he had met me, and I had shared how hard it was to get around anywhere in Malta. What he shared explained a lot about people not encountering wheelchairs.

At some event, I was sitting with Mario's Mum, and I'm pretty sure she knew I had a crush on him because he was so lovely to me and an adorable person. Mario's Mum commented, "Mario is always nice to people in wheelchairs." It hurt a lot because I wanted him to see me as Martha. I would love to ask Mario about that first encounter and if there was any chemistry. Suppose he saw past the wheelchair? I also wonder if his parents said he could only have a friendship with me. Who knows?

Mario and I remained friends even when I went back home. We wrote to each other.

Mario and my cousin, Sue, came and represented Malta in the 2000 Olympic Games held in Sydney. I got to watch them race in the hundred-metre heats. Andrew and I also got to go and pick them up and bring them over for lunch. All the family came and visited.

Neither Peter nor I could live in Malta. There was no wheelchair access or facilities I could use to make a life of it. Pete just never fit in.

Back home, life was so much easier: wheelchair taxis, ramps to everywhere, and accessible bathrooms.

When I came back to Australia, I started studying at TAFE again. I became terrific friends with this lady. She invited me to spend weekends with her and her husband in the city. After a couple of years, I was in my bed at their place, my friend was in the shower, and her husband came and kissed me. It was my first kiss. A passionate kiss that came out of the blue. I was not expecting him to kiss me, and once we started kissing, my body did not want to stop. My head told me this was not a good idea but, ultimately, my body won that battle. I was twenty-four when I had my first kiss, which was epic!

I knew it was wrong, as he was married to my friend, but I wanted this intimacy that I had dreamed about and my body screamed out for. I went on talking to him over the phone for three months. At that time, we met up once. At some point, I woke up to myself and realised that I deserved more from a relationship, and I ended it. Sadly, I never saw or spoke to them again. The guilt I felt, having stepped over the line with her husband, meant I could never see my friend again. A friendship was lost.

The floodgates opened once I had my first real kiss, and I could have other boyfriends.

There was another guy I met who I went out with for about one month, but that got old quickly. In his past relationships, the women had scammed him out of his money, and he wanted to take control of my money. He also wanted me to change and be 'more beautiful' by having long hair and nails, and wearing makeup. I wanted someone to love me for me. I said, "See ya later, alligator."

Around 1997, the internet and chatting with people online became a thing. I started talking to a guy named Tom. I was aware of all the dangers of giving my contact details. Tom asked me out, and I remember conversing with my parents about not wanting to give my details to a guy who wanted to ask me out. Dad said, "Just give him our address, we will be here." I gave Tom my address, and he picked me up, and we went out. Our relationship was developing, and we decided to be boyfriend and girlfriend, and a week later, it was all over. I was heartbroken and needed to know why. Tom had shared with his dad that he was going out with a girl in a wheelchair, and his dad told him not to get involved with someone in a wheelchair as it would be too much 'trouble.' His dad had not even met me. I was even more heartbroken after hearing that. Tom wanted to remain friends, but I did not wish to be friends. I wanted a full-on relationship where my love for another was reciprocated. I wanted to be kissed passionately and touched in adoring ways. I wanted to be loved for my intelligence and everything I was, minus my wheelchair and my disability. I did not want to be friends with a guy I had deep feelings for.

I swore off guys...and...a week later, I met Andrew!

I met Andrew at university in the room they had set up for people with disabilities to use — different computer set-ups, different tables, etc. There was an art exhibition that night, and Andrew offered to pick me up and take me. Andrew picked me up from home, was given the wheelchair packing and unpacking tutorial from Mum, and took me to the art exhibition where we had a good time, except the wheel on my wheelchair kept falling off. Andrew wanted to fix it, being the engineer that he is. I found this quite annoying as he did not even know me and he was touching my wheelchair, invading my personal space.

When Andrew drove me home that night, Dad asked me in Maltese if I wanted to invite him in for pizza. I said, "No," because he annoyed me so much. It comes in handy having another language you can communicate in at times. My parents and I speak in Maltese a lot. My parents could tell us off or tell us not to do something in Maltese in front of our Aussie friends and not embarrass us. It is great!

I still saw Andrew on and off at university. Andrew then shared that he had a girlfriend from church. I remember going home and sharing with my sister, Ruth, that there was a guy at university who now had a girlfriend and that I liked him.

The relationship with the girl was short-lived, and I swooped in to pick up the pieces. We hung out as friends for about nine months. I loved his mind, and he shared how my broken wheel bothered him. He did end up pulling the wheel apart and fixing it.

In the ninth month of our friendship, we became boyfriend and girlfriend. Andrew says he was leaning in for a hug, and I kissed him, but I think he intended to kiss me all along. Neither one of us will budge from our version of how our first kiss happened.

Soon after we became boyfriend and girlfriend, we knew we wanted to marry each other. Andrew took me to visit his parents, who seemed okay with me. Very early on in the relationship, I asked Andrew's Mum, Jean, if she had any issues with me being in a wheelchair and going out with her son. She responded, "No, not at all, should I?" I then went on to explain that the other boy's parents had not liked the idea that I was going out with their son as I was in a wheelchair. Jean responded, "As long as you make my son happy, that's all that matters!" I made Andrew smile a lot.

Andrew and I are complete opposites in every way possible. Andrew has fair hair, blue eyes, and fair skin. I have dark brown hair, brown eyes, and olive skin. Andrew is tall. I am short. I am very outgoing and like to laugh and be around people because I come from a big, contemporary Maltese family. Andrew likes quiet and comes from a small, conservative Australian family.

I started attending church with Andrew when we started going out. Andrew went to a Protestant church, and I was brought up Catholic. Dad had a little objection to attending a Protestant church, but Mum said it was still the same God, so he let me go. Mum and Dad ingrained in us our Catholic faith; however, we did not go to church every week or have friends within the congregation. Andrew went to church every week, and he had many church friends. It would have been crazy for us to start going to the Catholic church and start making friends again just because Dad said so. Going to church with Andrew made more sense, as the routine was already set and his friend group was already in place.

Andrew and I have the same values regarding finances, how to run a house, love, marriage, and sitting at the table to eat.

I have never had any issues with any of Andrew's family in regard to me being in a wheelchair. His parents, siblings, aunts, and uncles have embraced me as part of the family. I have been super lucky.

I always thought I was going to marry a Christian man. It was a feeling I had deep within me that I cannot explain. Perhaps it was a seed God planted a long time ago.

Andrew always felt that he would marry someone in a wheelchair, as that is the vision God gave him. As a joke, I often asked him, "What, like an old lady?" It is wild how you have an innate, unexplainable idea that forms with no rhyme or reason.

When Andrew and I were getting serious about spending the rest of our lives together, I needed to know if Andrew could do twenty-four-seven with me. We decided to go to Canberra for a week. It was cold even though it was the middle of summer. Andrew did a great job helping me with personal care, eating, drinking, and getting me from A to B. We had a great time together, and I felt Andrew could manage me.

Nine months after being boyfriend and girlfriend, Andrew took Mum and Dad out to dinner and asked them if he could marry me. They said, "Yes!" Dad said he wanted two cows and a donkey to let Andrew marry me.

That night, Andrew stayed up all night and braided together a copper ring. The next day, I had to get up early and go out with Andrew. He took me to a spot in the mountains to catch the first bit of sunrise, where he proposed to me with the ring he had made me. I said, "Yes!"

In Pursuit...

- I just wanted to be seen for who I was.

- I finally found the one who saw me for myself and my extras as benefits, not hurdles.

- When the relationship is right, it works.

Me and Mario in 1993

What Mario wrote in my autograph book in 1993

What Mario wrote in my autograph book in 2000

Andrew and me

Chapter 8

Marriage is Harder than Getting a Degree

Marriage is Looong

The next time Andrew and his parents visited Mum and Dad, they presented Dad with a cow and a donkey made of ceramic. These were close enough for Dad to let me marry Andrew — phew!

Andrew and I both enjoyed setting up our wedding. We did not argue about any of it. Andrew picked the flowers for me with the help of the florist. I was very fussy about the stationery we used to have the invitations made, but I finally found the right ones.

Mum designed my wedding dress and haggled down the price. My only request was that the top had cheeky sleeves. My wedding dress was made for me. It was a two-piece, a skirt and top ensemble.

My Dad did not like the building we would be getting married in, which was the church we were attending. Six weeks before our actual wedding, we were looking for a new church to be married at. We found one with the one date we needed and booked it in.

As well as setting up the wedding, we went house hunting to have somewhere to live after marriage. In case we had to have renovations done, we started looking early.

The houses we were shown were horrendous, in that most could not get a wheelchair in the front door. After two days of looking, I wanted to give up. We decided to change the way we approached looking for houses. We went to about five real estate agents and told them our specifications. One guy rang out of the five agents and said, "I have the perfect house for you." We visited the property in our preferred area, which was relatively flat, and I fit through the front door. The only modification the house needed for me to manage was to widen the bathroom doorway, which Dad could do as a carpenter — SOLD! Twenty-five years later, we are still in the house. We did have concrete paths built around the house, a garage added, and a back patio.

Dad wanted to make sure we had nice furniture in our formal lounge and dining rooms, so he took me furniture shopping. We found a furniture set, and Dad wanted me to buy it there and then on the spot. I slowed him down a bit by asking Andrew to see it first. Andrew also liked it. Twenty-five years later, we still have the furniture.

Before we were married, we thought it would be nice to have some professional photos taken to give to our parents as a thank-you gift for giving us the wedding. We had to take a few nice outfits to the venue to get dressed and have the photos taken. As we took my clothes from home, Mum wanted to know what we were doing. I could not tell her as it was a surprise for her. Mum was very angry at me and said, "How dare you keep secrets from me!" I thought this was hilarious! On the wedding day, as we presented our parents with the framed photos; Mum shared that she thought we were taking the nice outfits from the house to go and elope. I responded, "I went to all this trouble to arrange the wedding; why would I have eloped?"

Six months before we got married, we had the opportunity to go to Malta for a holiday so that Andrew could meet the rest of the family. My cousin Christian was getting married, so I ensured our time in Malta coincided with his wedding. Christian and Stefania married in July 1999, and we married in December 1999. My family in Malta all got to meet Andrew. They were mesmerised by his fair hair and blue eyes. I had found a catch!

Andrew and I both had some trepidation around living together after marriage. Our worries were around feeding each other and keeping the house and yard clean and tidy.

I was concerned about the area of sex. Could I do it? Would I like it? The tension of not knowing was driving me crazy. Three weeks before we were due to be married, we did IT! It was okay, and I could manage it all. After we did it that first time, I was ready for some spooning and cuddles, but Andrew was very disappointed that we did not wait until our wedding night...

We were determined to make our marriage work, and we did. After we were married, we were assessed for Homecare. The assessment took a couple of months to be done. It took another couple of months to have a domestic assistant dedicated to us. After six to nine months, we had one and a half hours a week of someone coming in to help us clean the house — yay!

Andrew struggled with making our dinners around the three-year mark of marriage. He was just getting slower and slower, and I was getting depressed. We were also starting our IVF journey at this time, and the stress of it all made Andrew's ability to get things done that much harder.

Around Christmas time, an organisation was wrapping gifts at the shops. In addition to offering gift wrapping, other flyers advertised their services. I shared that I needed more help at home, and they gave me a number to call. I met with a case worker who organised a person to come in one hour daily to prepare and feed me breakfast and prepare our evening meals. This help was invaluable.

Another area of dispute was the lawns. I wanted them to

be kept neat, but Andrew hated this job. We constantly fought over when it needed mowing and how well it was done. Finally, I outsourced the job, as the money I paid for the lawns to be done also paid for less conflict.

Andrew and I only really fought over the lawns and how neat the house was. There were no real dramas as I could keep the inside of the house tidy.

I would put everything that Andrew left lying around the house that was his into his office. I realised I needed my own office very early on, as sharing with Andrew would have been a nightmare. I would have spent my whole time tidying up after Andrew and not gotten any of my work done.

The way Andrew and I work in our offices is entirely different. I have a very organised, clean, spacious, and colourful room. Andrew's office is very industrial, with many bits and pieces around it, and it looks like an engineering workshop. I am glad I knew what I was getting into with office spaces and thought ahead to have my own room.

Andrew and I like living together. We are both easy to get along with. I have good communication skills, and we often head in the right direction.

After receiving more help throughout the week for many years, I was at a workshop where I met this beautiful lady, Elle, who had a support worker. I was intrigued, and I decided to ask how this all worked.

Before NDIS, there was CSP, Community Support Program, where people with high levels of disability were assessed and given packages to do daily life with. I investigated it, and I was evaluated and approved for funding. I then had to find an organisation to manage my money and pay my bills. I had no idea where to look for such an organisation. Eventually, I rang the funding body and asked them what to do. The lady I spoke to was kind enough to point me to an organisation that was not on the list but was the perfect fit for me.

Living My Way was the first organisation to pilot CSP.

I was in safe hands and was shown how to use my funding and hire Support workers to be more independent. My package was rolled over to NDIS three years after being on CSP. Together with Living My Way, we figured out this new terrain, with its language and boundaries. My support did not have to change much between CSP and NDIS; the only real difference was the different categories the money had to be taken out of. Instead of having one pot of money for everything, I now have pots of money for various things.

NDIS has a lot more red tape and hurdles to jump over, which is hard when trying to get on with life, work, and run a family.

In addition to applying for CSP, I decided to fundraise to get a wheelchair-accessible vehicle, one where my power wheelchair could roll up into the back so I could go out with my support worker.

I had a team of friends who taught me how to fundraise and point me in the right direction. Fundraising is hard work. It is much like having a job. I sent out letters, did some public speaking, had a raffle, put together a fundraising dinner, and had money tins everywhere. I accomplished my goal of raising enough money to buy a car, and I was going to start fundraising for the conversion when a miracle happened.

Andrew and I went to the car dealership on a Monday to check on the price of the car. The salesman went to get us some water, and when he came back, he shared with us that someone had just traded in a fully converted wheelchair-accessible vehicle in nearly brand-new condition. The price was that of a new car! I had the money to buy the car. Job done! The car is called the Venga Bus.

Andrew and I have always created a positive culture where we can live together. We always step up to help each other through the highs and lows. My family all live very close, five to twenty minutes away, and are always on hand.

In the early days, Andrew would visit his parents for a

week, and I would go home to my parents every couple of months just for a break and a refresh.

Dad often dropped in for a cuppa or to help if Andrew was unwell. When Dad passed away, I missed him. Now that my Mum is in her eighties, she finds it hard to look after me, so we do not ask her much.

Andrew's parents live one and a half hours away and are more like guests when they come over. However, they often take us out to lunch and dinner when they visit, which removes a lot of stress.

Andrew and I stick to a budget and always pay our bills on time.

Andrew and I love going on holidays together. Andrew books a lot of our cruises.

Sex has gotten easier as we have gotten older. About five years ago, I could get to a point of orgasm where the palms of your hands and the soles of your feet tingle — it is quite the sensation. I talked to a colleague at work and asked her if she experienced these tingles. She did! As code, we would ask each other, "Have you had any Fruit Tingles lately?" We would laugh and laugh. She bought me a bag of Fruit Tingles for Christmas with five packs of lollies inside. I immediately opened the bag and gave her some in case she had an emergency and needed some Fruit Tingles. We still laugh when we catch up.

As Andrew and I got older, we enjoyed being home more. We live in a lovely, spacious, clutter-free, relaxing space. The comforts of home life are enough. We live with our dog Bronte and have a few plants in our house and on the back patio. A few friends we see from time to time, and we use video calls to stay in contact with others.

Life is good, and I am getting stronger and returning to my old self daily.

Marriage is more challenging than getting a degree — the years are more prolonged, and two lives are on the line, not just one. I was able to quit university and not have it impact anyone. I often compare marriage and university because I met Andrew at university, and I did not get a degree, but I got a great husband.

Andrew and I might look like we are having an easy life, but we are like ducks. We look calm on the surface, but we are paddling hard underneath.

I feel that although people are accepting of my disability, they do not know what it takes for me to get ready for the day. After being in a coma, I do need more help as my capacity to be as independent as I used to has diminished. Asking Andrew to help me more is taxing both mentally and physically.

Since my coma, my ability to cope mentally with day-to-day life has gotten more complex. I get overwhelmed and tired a lot quicker.

In Pursuit...

- Communication is the key.

- Andrew and I look after each other as best we can. I am the brains, Andrew is the brawn, and sometimes, he is the brains, too!

- I married well.

On our wedding day

Our family: Pupa, me, Bronte, Andrew, and Pixie

Chapter 9
Oh, Baby, Baby

When I was twenty-nine years old, my biological clock started ticking. Andrew still had a year left of university, so we decided to wait another year before trying.

For my thirtieth birthday, we went on a holiday to Daydream Island, and I planned to come home pregnant. That did not happen.

Month two of trying, I got my period; month three of trying, I got my period again. I thought I would be pregnant like all the other women in my family by now. After eight months of trying to get pregnant, I felt that there was something wrong.

I had seen an obstetrician/gynaecologist, Doctor Murray, at our local hospital after we were married, who specialised in helping women with special needs to deliver babies. I went to see him to check if it was okay for me to have a baby with my disability. After chatting, he said, "I'll see you when you are pregnant."

I made an appointment to see Doctor Murray. When Andrew and I saw him, I shared that we had been trying to conceive for eight months, and nothing had happened. Doctor Murray assured me that if I felt something was wrong, it was time for us to get tested. Andrew and I both had blood tests, and Andrew had to have his sperm tested.

We did all the tests we had to do, then waited for our next appointment to see Doctor Murray.

I was not ready for what Doctor Murray had to say. I was sure something was wrong with me, but there was not. Doctor Murray shared that Andrew had a meagre sperm count and the only way for us to get pregnant was to do a form of IVF — in vitro fertilisation — called ICSI — intracytoplasmic sperm injection — where they inject Andrew's sperm into one of my eggs.

I was devastated by the news. I went home and cried and cried. I had always dreamed of having a baby, like my sisters, and I was just told that it was impossible to conceive a child naturally. My heart broke, and this news changed something in me forever.

Andrew was not keen to do IVF, and we both thought that the price of IVF would be out of our grasp. I, we, had to absorb the news of the inability to conceive naturally and make some peace with it before looking at anything to do with IVF.

After a couple of months, I went to my local GP to get a referral to see an IVF specialist at Westmead Hospital.

The specialist was great and very sympathetic to what I would now endure to get pregnant. He thoroughly examined Andrew in case there was a quick fix to the issue, but sadly, nothing, so through IVF we had to go.

My mental health had taken a beating with the shock of not being able to fall pregnant naturally. I was too scared to say anything to anyone as I was worried that I would be seen as an unfit parent or that it was no longer safe for me to do IVF.

To do IVF, we had to meet with a fertility counsellor. She gave us a good tip: Do not look too far into the future. Focus on what you can do today. This tip has helped me through many hard times. Other than that, I do not think I gelled with the counsellor and did not want to see her again.

The first round of IVF was unknown. Each step was a new

step. Even though I tried to prepare myself for different scenarios, the outcome would still differ.

To start an IVF cycle, I had to be on the pill. Once I got my period, on a particular day I had to start taking a medicine I squirted up my nose so no eggs were released into my next cycle. This medicine had to be taken every twelve hours. On a particular day, I had to start having an injection in my tummy to produce lots of eggs. An internal ultrasound was done to see how many eggs were in each ovary and the next step of the cycle. My first cycle of IVF ended there as I was overstimulated. I produced over thirty-six eggs. This was very dangerous as my ovaries could have ruptured. I was told to go home and stop all medications. I was devastated! I had to ring the nurse and ask what happened to all my eggs? My body would absorb them.

All the medication I had to have for IVF had to be administered to me by Andrew as I physically did not have the fine motor skills to do it myself. Andrew was very good at administering the medications. It was nice that we were doing this together, but it was also sad that I could not just do it alone and be done with it.

I was the one who had to keep the atmosphere light and happy while I felt that Andrew just disapproved.

Andrew's stand on having babies was that if God wanted to give us a child, he would. I did not think this was right as there was a problem, and IVF was available for us to try. This discord was underlying all the years we tried to have a baby. This was very disheartening and exhausting.

I then had to wait another two months to start the next cycle.

Each cycle took about seven weeks. I believe it is much shorter now. In the second cycle, I went through the medicine up my nose and then the injections with a much lesser dose.

When my eggs were 'cooked' I had to be given an injection by a nurse thirty-six hours before collection. I had a 3pm collection, which meant I had to be given my injection at 3am. Luckily, I had a friend who was a nurse who was willing to sleep over, wake up, and give me the injection. My friend told me I was too old to have a baby. I was thirty-one years old. She gave me my injection to respect my wishes.

Everyone had an opinion on my wanting to have a baby. If I had gotten pregnant naturally, they would have just been happy for me. I just wanted and needed encouragement. It is such a trauma to find out you have to do IVF. Doing IVF in itself is a trauma. When you want a baby badly enough, you will try anything. Dad encouraged me, but not many other people.

On the day of egg collection, Andrew had to give his sperm to the lab. I produced about eighteen eggs, which was a good harvest. It made me feel like I was a chicken laying lots of eggs. For my eggs to be collected, I was put under sedation. The number of eggs collected is written on your hand so you can see it when you wake up. The nurse asked, "Do you have any abdominal pain or discomfort?" I said, "Yes." I was given morphine. I started vomiting and I could not stop. Because it was late, the nurses got me in my chair, gave me a vomit bag, and sent me home. We were staying at a hotel across the road. I did not stop vomiting until around 11pm. I now know that I am allergic to morphine.

The next part in the process of getting pregnant was to enter a pessary into your vagina every twelve hours. Again, I could not do this myself, and Andrew had to do it.

Andrew's sperm and my eggs were joined in the lab and left to 'hatch.' The day after egg collection, I rang the lab to see how many embryos were viable. Out of my eighteen eggs inseminated, six were viable the next day. I had to have blood tests to know when a good time would be to implant an embryo into my uterus. Another injection needed to be given to give a synthetic version of hCG — human chorionic gonadotropin — into my body so that my body felt pregnant and would take on the embryo and nurture it to become a baby, hopefully. Out of my eighteen eggs, six became embryos. On the day of the transfer, we had one embryo left, which was transferred into my uterus.

To keep me comfortable to do the embryo transfer, I was given an intravenous relaxant. The embryo was then transferred. I was sent home to keep doing the pessaries. I then had to wait. I was waiting to either get my period or get up to the day of doing the blood test and find out I was pregnant.

I got my period. I was not pregnant. I was devastated. I would have to do IVF from the beginning if I wanted to try again.

I had a lot to think about.

The whole ordeal of trying to get pregnant felt like a tug-of-war between God and science. Some people had the perspective that God created these scientists who could assist women with getting pregnant through IVF, so was that not also the will of God?

After two rounds of IVF, I needed to take a break, as I did not think Andrew and I wanted the same thing in the same way. I felt dragged down and disheartened. In my heart, I wanted a baby, but in my mind, I felt resistance. I felt that people in the family judged whether I could manage to have a baby and whether Andrew would cope with the sound of a baby crying.

Dad was my biggest cheerleader through all this. Dad believed I could do anything I set my mind to, and he understood I wanted to be like everyone else. I, too, wanted to be a mother.

My mental health had taken a beating. I was depressed, but I was scared to get help because I felt that I would be considered unfit to try IVF again or even to be a mother.

I felt alone. I feel like I stared at a wall for two years and just went through the motions of life. I did not taste anything, and there was no joy in anything I did. I know I read books but did not absorb anything I read.

I remember always thinking that my house was a mess and that everything in my house was out of control.

Whenever Mum and Dad visited, I would ask if my house was a mess. Mum always assured me that my house was tidy.

After about six months, I convinced Andrew to try IVF again. The process of making lots of eggs went smoothly. I made around twenty-four eggs, six of which became embryos. One embryo was transferred, and one embryo was frozen.

Again, I got my period before getting to do the pregnancy blood test. I was not pregnant; however, I did have a frozen embryo, so I would not have to go through the whole IVF process again.

To transfer a frozen embryo, my hormones had to be suppressed and controlled. I had to take certain medications and then have a lot of blood tests to get my hormones to a level that would create a suitable environment for an embryo to attach and develop into a baby.

Once my hormone levels were correct, the frozen embryo was thawed and watched to see if it was viable for transfer. The lab rang on the morning of the day of the transfer to let me know that the embryo had not survived overnight and that the transfer was not going to take place.

I hoped this could start a new chapter in my life, and one phone call crumbled my hopes.

I decided to do back-to-back cycles, so I started another cycle as soon as possible. Everything was going smoothly. The day before my egg collection, Andrew got a twenty-four-hour bug that gave him vomiting and fever. The fever was not good for sperm as it could inhibit the very few sperm that were there to begin with.

I rang the clinic and was told I had two options. I could stop the cycle there and then, six weeks in, start another cycle, or we could keep going and see what happens. I decided we would keep going as I was done after this cycle — the egg collection produced over fifteen eggs. Twelve of them had sperm injected into them, and the lab rang to tell me that due to the poor quality of the sperm, my remaining eggs were not put in a petri dish with any sperm as their motility was too poor.

The next day, we rang the lab and were told we had six embryos. On the day of embryo transfer, we had two embryos. One was transferred into my uterus, and the other embryo was frozen.

Again, I got my period before I went for the pregnancy blood test — another disappointment.

I left it a few months before having the frozen embryo inserted. I called and booked in once I gathered my strength and guts to try again. My hormones were prepared, and the embryo defrosted and kept developing. The embryo transfer seemed set to go ahead, as we did not hear from the lab.

We made our way to our local train station, hopped on the train, and before we reached the next stop, we received a call from the lab to say that there was no point in going to the clinic as our embryo had died.

I felt empty and had to figure out our next move rather quickly. We jumped off the train at the next stop and met my parents at the shops.

I went around the shops with my parents in a state of shock. I was not ready to receive that kind of news in a moving vehicle. I was shattered. We returned to my parent's place for lunch, and then Dad drove us back to the station to collect our car.

Once we got home, the house was just eerily silent. Andrew went into his office and shut the door. I was left all on my own, and I was numb. I decided that I wanted to die. I wrote a letter in my notebook. I got a bottle of port and twenty Panadol. If I had the Panadol and port, I would sleep and never wake up again. I saw no point in going on when my dream of having a baby was so out of my reach and grasp. Life sucked, and I felt so rejected by Andrew that I did not want to go on. There was so much pain in feeling nothingness and numbness.

I took the Panadol with the port and I laid down. It took me a couple of hours to go to sleep. Every couple of hours, I would wake up, go to the toilet and vomit. Eight hours after arriving home, Andrew came to bed.

I was mad and sad that he did not check on me or ask me if I wanted a cup of tea or something to eat. I knew I had made the right decision to take my life. Andrew was sick of me and my baby antics.

I slept through the night, and in the morning, I unfortunately woke up.

I told Andrew what I had done in the morning, and he hit the roof. The hospital is about ten minutes away from where we live. Andrew drove me to the emergency room, and they took me straight in and put me on a drip to get the poison out of my system.

While I was admitted, Andrew rang our parents and told them where I was. When Mum and Dad came to visit, Dad shared with me that he could see that I had been troubled the day before, having gotten the news that my embryo had not survived while I was on the train.

The medicine that I was given via the drip at the hospital caused me to vomit. Tests showed that the Panadol I had taken had not damaged my liver.

The hospital psychiatrist saw me, and she asked, "Why did you want to end your life?" I replied, "I want to have a baby." She asked, "Why do you want to have a baby?" I replied, "It is a piece of the puzzle missing in my life."

After staying overnight in the emergency room, the doctors discussed if I was to go into the hospital's mental health facility. It was decided that I would go home and have the outpatient mental health care team visit me at home.

Andrew's Mum and Dad stayed with us for a couple of days. I did not want to be at home alone with Andrew as I did not want to be left alone by him. Having more people in the house helped fill the silence.

After being home one day, the outpatient mental health care team came to visit me. They assessed that I would not need another visit as I had family around. They gave me a card with a number to ring if I needed to talk. I also promised that I would make an appointment to see my counsellor.

I was shocked by what I had done, and people rang on the home phone to see if I was okay. I answered the phone a lot and assured them that I was alright.

When I saw my counsellor, he asked, "Why are you smiling?" My response was, "I am in shock." I did not know how I was going to get over the devastation that my plans for having a baby were over.

I was not going to be doing IVF again, and I also knew that there was not going to be any miracle to get me pregnant. I was going to remain childless.

I was in total despair and felt that there was no hope in sight. My heart was broken, and I felt a lot of emotional pain.

Andrew decided that we needed to go on a holiday to get a change of scenery.

We booked a holiday to the Gold Coast, where we stayed for a week. We stayed at the Watermark Hotel. Just outside the door, there were three churches. I felt called to go to Surf City Church that Sunday. As the service started, there was a baby dedication, and I thought, "What am I doing here?" As the service continued, I learned that this church specialised in praying for couples who could not have children, as we were visiting this church for the first time; after the service, we were taken to an area where newcomers are met. I shared our heartbreak in trying to have children. The senior pastor was called to pray over us. The prayer lifted the hopelessness off me, and I felt whole again. God had healed my heart. After the holiday, we went home, and I felt like a new woman.

I got into my art and did volunteer work. I worked on making peace with not having children and focusing on other areas of my life.

Very soon after this, we got our first dog, Pupa.

About seven years later, Dad passed away. My siblings and I supported Mum in putting together Dad's funeral service and his wake. As a family, we worked harmoniously and were there for each other.

I reflected on this a lot and felt that I needed to try IVF again. I wanted to have someone to bury me.

As I was forty-two years old, I could no longer go through the public hospital system. The public hospital only assists couples who are under the age of forty.

I had met a lady through Toastmasters who raved about a clinic in Hurstville that she had used.

I rang and got the ball rolling on what we had to do to do IVF through the clinic. Things had changed quite a bit since I had last done a cycle.

We met with a female doctor who was very happy to try to help us get pregnant. The facility was set up like a day spa and had no hint of looking like a hospital, which was very nice.

I had to get a copy of my records sent to my new clinic. We then had a series of blood tests and urine tests done. I had to have an ultrasound of my uterus.

All the tests were to see if we were deficient in any vitamins. We had to go onto some vitamins to give my eggs and Andrew's sperm the best possible chance of being healthy. My ultrasound showed a very healthy uterus.

We started a cycle after a few months of being on the vitamins.

One issue I had was that I was prescribed a higher dose to produce lots of eggs. I immediately rang and asked the nurses to double-check with the doctor what dose I had to be on. The dose was halved, and I was happy with it.

The cycle went smoothly after that. I made lots of eggs, and the egg pick-up went well.

Out of twelve eggs, we again had six embryos; one was

implanted, and two were frozen.

I got to the pregnancy blood test before getting my period. The blood test on Friday was inconclusive. I had no idea what inconclusive meant. I thought it was a dud reading, and I was distraught that I was not told if I was pregnant or not.

The following Monday, I still had not gotten my period, but the blood test showed that I was not pregnant. I asked when my period would come, and the nurse said, "Soon." Within a week, it came on.

A month later, we decided to have the two frozen embryos transferred into my uterus. They both remained viable, so I decided to have them both implanted. I guess I was being defiant to Andrew and his Mum in putting two embryos in, as they were so against it. I did not want to go through the frozen embryo transfer twice as it was rather gruelling. I also thought that by having two transferred, one might keep the other alive, and I might have a better chance of getting pregnant with one baby.

As it turned out, I was not pregnant.

When I first decided to go to this clinic, I was hoping to use a sperm donor. After much discussion with Andrew, we decided to try using Andrew's sperm in the first cycle, and if I did not get pregnant, we would try using a sperm donor for the second cycle.

The whole donor area is enormous. At the clinic, the sperm bank has Australian and American donors. The Australian donor bank gave a lot less information on the donors because Australia has a smaller population, and there is a greater chance that you may discover who the donor is. There was also a smaller number of times Australian sperm could impregnate a woman. This would also be so that the sperm donor would not have ten children inbreeding with one another when they became adults. Donor sperm was a huge minefield. But still, I continued.

I reviewed the Australian and American databases, compiled my top five list, and returned it to the clinic.

I went through another cycle and had my egg transfer, then had my eggs inseminated with the donor sperm. When I went for the embryo transfer, I had one embryo implanted and five embryos frozen.

The cycle was very stressful, and my body ached all over. Looking back, I now know it was because I felt so stressed about doing something so 'different.'

Being home with the embryo inside me made me feel yucky. It made me feel like I had cheated on Andrew. I guess you do not realise the feelings you will feel until you are in a particular situation.

As it turned out, I was not pregnant. We kept the five frozen embryos at the clinic for six months, and then we decided to let them go.

I did not think my body could go through IVF anymore. I gave it six good goes. I had had enough emotional pain, physical trauma, and lots and lots of disappointments.

I have no regrets.

I will always mourn that I never had a child, and I do not think I will ever be fully happy, but those are the cards you are dealt with in life, and you have to put one foot in front of the other and keep walking forward.

In Pursuit...

- You can only try your best in complex situations and learn what you can from your hard times.

- Hard times help you to grow if you let them.

- "You can be bitter or better, but you can't be both." — Joyce Meyer.

Chapter 10
Our Dogs

A Dog is a Friend for Life!

After trying to have a baby, Andrew and I had talked on and off about getting a dog. When Andrew was at boarding school, he had a housemaster with a cavalier King Charles spaniel. Andrew often spoke about how lovely the dog was and how he would like that breed.

A friend at church needed to rehome her dog, so we agreed to take him on. Buster was a big beagle, and when he came home, I quickly learned that he was too much of a dog for me. We returned Buster to his previous owners after twenty-four hours, and we decided to wait a bit longer before getting a dog.

My friend, Vanessa, was going away for a few days, so we offered to look after her cavalier King Charles spaniel, Winchester. We fell in love with him.

We learned that Mum's friend, Josephine, had a litter of Maltese pups crossed with a cavalier. The pups were Maltaliers. We contacted Josephine and arranged to meet the puppies. One scraggly girl was in the litter.

This puppy was ours. We paid our deposit. I waited until she was eight weeks old, collected her, and brought her home. She vomited in the car on the way home as she was a bit carsick.

We called her 'Pupa,' which means 'beautiful doll' in Maltese.

Andrew and I had no idea what to do with this little dog. We gave her puppy food and water. Mum suggested we give her a raw egg. After tasting it, Pupa started heaving and vomiting, and I freaked out. My niece, Leeanne, came over and assured us that Pupa was okay.

I went to the bathroom, and Pupa followed me and peed on the floor. It was adorable.

When Pupa was old enough, we took her to puppy preschool, and she was terrific. On our first visit, Pupa sat at my front wheel. The instructor was amazed and told us what a great dog we had.

At puppy preschool, we taught Pupa to sit, come, stay. We learned that we had to control Pupa's barking. We taught her not to bark when it was dark. We were also advised to get a playpen so Pupa could have her area.

Pupa was a great dog. Pupa taught us everything we needed to know.

Pupa was happy to follow us around and be next to us.

Pupa loved putting her head between my front and back wheel to sleep. Pupa instinctively knew when I would move and got out of the way. I never ran her over.

What we found peculiar with Pupa was that at 11pm, she would get this energy and go pelting around the house for half an hour, come back to bed, and sleep. We tried stopping her a few times but quickly discovered that letting her get it out of her system was easier. We called this 'the fun runs.'

Pupa was uncoordinated as a puppy. Pupa would lie against the side of her bed, somehow topple over, and end up with the bed on top of her. We would think she looked like a turtle and laugh at her.

As a puppy, Pupa would put her head over the side of our concrete veranda, a small step, and her body would topple over her head. We would often say, "Oh, Pupa, are you okay?"

At four months, we took Pupa on a road trip to Melbourne. Pupa slept in her bed in the car and would wake up every two hours. She wanted to pee and go for a little walk. She behaved well on the way there and back and while we were in Melbourne. Family and friends could not believe we took a puppy on a road trip.

Pupa is a social dog and loves being around people. She learned very early that the best vantage point to reach up to people and kiss them was on my lap when they leaned in to kiss me.

When Andrew and I go out, upon returning home, Pupa jumps up on my lap, puts a front paw on each of my shoulders, and kisses my face. I give her a big hug and tell her I love her. Andrew then picks her up off my lap and hugs her. Her unconditional love is unfathomable.

Pupa also loved to bite my socks off my feet as a puppy. To her, it was a game, but sharp puppy teeth hurt. I once went to Mum's crying and in pain, with band-aids on my toes as they were bleeding. I tried giving Pupa other socks that were not on my feet, and we also got a pair of Andrew's old socks and hid a treat in the rolled-up sock for her to master unrolling and finding the treat. Pupa enjoyed these puzzles and soon forgot about my feet.

Pupa loves having toys and likes playing with them, taking them for a walk, wrestling with them, and lying amongst them.

Pupa's hair is white and caramel. Her hair was scraggly, especially her tail, but we loved her heaps. Her hair grew stronger and thicker as she was groomed every six months. The trainer shared that washing her would cause skin irritations. We learned that because Pupa was such a clean dog, she did not need to be bathed and that her natural oils kept her clean if we fed her well. Occasionally, Pupa would get muddy feet or dirty ears, so we just washed what needed cleaning.

During the day, Pupa spent time with me, following me around and sleeping with her head between my front and back wheels. At night, Pupa slept against Andrew. Because Pupa followed me so closely, under the back of my wheelchair, when I turned round to see her behind me, all I could see was her tail. In that position, I called her 'My Tail.'

At six months, Pupa started getting quiet, and Andrew decided it was time to get another dog. Because Pupa was such a great breed, we wanted the same breed in our next dog.

We learnt that Josephine had pups again. We visited Josephine and met this cute little fluff ball with a big bottom.

Before we went to meet our new puppy, Andrew and I were discussing names. We settled on the name Phoebe. Phoebe had slipped our minds when we met this three-week-old big-bottomed pup, so I asked, "How about Bronte?" And Bronte, she is. Bronte had to stay with Josephine until she was eight weeks old, but we snuck in another visit. She was the size of my hand at the first visit and, at the second visit, the length of my forearm. When Bronte came home, she was the size of both my hand and forearm.

Bronte was different from Pupa; she was a lot fluffier and whiter, and had smaller patches of caramel. Bronte still had a more significant bottom. Bronte seemed to be a lot more coordinated than Pupa. When Bronte put her head over the side of the veranda, her body stayed on the veranda. Bronte could also lift and carry around bones as big as her. Pupa would not even attempt that.

Pupa mothered Bronte and taught her how to clean and keep herself. Pupa and Bronte also played together. Pupa would chase Bronte, Bronte would drop, and then Pupa would jump over her.

Pupa and Bronte were a great team. Bronte would lie on Pupa, and Pupa would just let her. They shared food, water, beds, and places.

One minute, you would see one dog in one spot and the other in another, then look again and see that they had swapped.

Bronte is not as affectionate or as social as Pupa. Bronte does what Pupa does. If we are out, upon coming home, Pupa will jump up and greet me, and then Bronte will do the same. We love our time with Pupa and Bronte.

Pupa is Andrew's dog and would happily get picked up and have more cuddles during the day.

Bronte is very much my dog. She wants stability and knows I am there for her. At night, I did not want to sleep with a dog against me because of my involuntary movements, but Bronte pushed those barriers nestled up against my tummy and put her head on my hip. We rarely sleep like this; Bronte will stay there for a bit, then go and find another spot to rest. Bronte still does this today. Bronte is not much of a lap dog. She likes to rest against you. She likes to lean on you and sleep.

We discovered that Bronte could burp loudly. As soon as we lay down for our afternoon nap, Bronte will eat her dried biscuits. After having her fill, she drinks water, lays on the bed, licks her chops, and gives us an almighty burp. We laugh every day at this. It is a ritual we both wait and hold our breath to hear.

Bronte burps more than she farts, which is lucky for us. Her first noisy fart scared the shit out of her. Bronte kept looking at her bottom and wondering what had happened. I am glad I was there to witness it. I thought it was so funny! I kept asking her, "What happened, Bronte?"

I wanted Pupa to have a litter of pups in place of me. However, after Pupa had her first coming into heat – 'period', I could not let her go through that trauma again. Pupa is a very clean dog, and having a period was too distressing for her, so after it was over, we booked both Pupa and Bronte to get desexed. They wore cones around their heads to avoid pulling their stitches out.

Having cone heads did not stop them from jumping up on my lap. Instead of one big jump, they got up on my footplates and calf strap then onto my lap. Pupa somehow reverse parks her bottom onto my lap.

My lap is the safest place for Bronte when the mowing is

done. Bronte hates the noise of the whipper snipper. Bronte now recognises the gardener knocking at the door and jumps onto my lap. It does not matter how often I put her on the lounge; she will get back on my lap, and if she could jump into my body to hide from the horrible noise, she would.

Our vet, Camille, bought the practice when Pupa was six months old. We became terrific friends with her as we supported her in attending her open days and voting for her in the local business awards. Camille is great at helping teach us about our dogs and how to look after them well. We have many laughs together, especially when taking Pupa and Bronte to see Camille. Camille often picks up the wrong dog to vaccinate! Camille now asks us to put the right dog on the examination table for her to treat.

Camille has her dogs, too. One of her dogs, Pony, won my heart — a big black dog with a paw the size of my hand but very gentle.

Pony and I are good friends because he got me into trouble one day by pretending he was my dog and following a lady with a cat inside. The lady looked at me and said, "You should have your dog on a leash!" I did, and they were also sitting on my lap. I said, "He's not my dog." Pony used to be let out the back to pee and sneak around the front to say "Hi" to everyone. Pony was edging closer to the front gate on this particular visit, so we thought it best to call him over to us.

Since that day, whenever I see Pony, I say, "Even though you got me into trouble, I still love you!" In COVID days, Camille brought Pony outside for him to say "Hi!" and he cocked his leg and peed on my wheelchair. See, I told you the love is mutual.

After about four years of having Pupa and Bronte, our friends on Facebook shared that they needed to rehome a dog they had as the place they were moving to had no fences. We replied that we would take her if no one else wanted her. Six months later, we met Pixie. Pixie is a Maltese cross Australian silky. I often joked that if Andrew and I had a baby, it would have looked like Pixie because I am Maltese and Andrew is Australian.

Pixie is all white with grey ears and a few grey spots on her body. Pixie has one set of black eyelashes and one set of white eyelashes. She is such an adorable dog. When we first introduced Pixie to my parents, Mum was furious as she thought Pixie would replace Pupa and Bronte, but that did not happen as Pixie needed her own space. Pixie ended up becoming Mum's favourite dog; she treats her like a baby, and Pixie laps it up.

When we took Pixie to meet Camille, Pixie was angry and bitey, and Camille asked, "What have you taken on?" A dog that needed desexing and an operation to have her dewclaws removed. I was a bit upset that there was such a negative response to us trying to do right by a dog. We had to change ownership and put Pixie into our name through the council. Once the paperwork went through, we discovered we had missed Pixie's birthday.

Pixie had been in five very different homes. The last home she was in, she was fed and watered but left outside twenty-four-seven. It took us two days to get her inside.

Anytime she felt threatened, she showed her teeth and growled. If anyone with black socks and shoes came through the house, Pixie would try to attack and bite the back of their heels. This was an obvious sign of trauma.

Pixie also jumped the gate when we were out or chewed the chicken wire and crawled out the bottom of the gate. Camille suggested we get her a dog crate while we were out. This worked, and after a couple of weeks in the crate, while we were out, she could stay in the backyard.

We found that the best way for Pixie to overcome her trauma was not through discipline but to massage her body and give her lots of physical contact and unconditional love.

Pixie was settling in well. At Easter time, Pixie found a box of Tim Tam Bites, dragged them under the bed, and proceeded to eat them one by one after tearing open each bite. I went to the bathroom and smelled chocolate. When I looked under the bed, I saw seven empty wrappers! Pixie had eaten seven Tim Tam Bites! I freaked out, as chocolate can kill dogs. It was too late to take Pixie to the vet, so we took her the next day.

I did not sleep well that night as I worried about Pixie. I kept checking her to see that she was still breathing. Fortunately, she was. In the morning, she was all swollen and blown up. She looked like a rugby ball. We rang Camille first thing and met her at the clinic. Pixie was given a tiny blue pill on the inside of her eyelid, and in about ten minutes, she started vomiting. The room smelled of Tim Tams. Pixie had to stay at the clinic for the day; her heart rate was double, and there was no guarantee that she would not have a heart attack and die. But the naughty little bugger pulled through. She is a tough little dog. A five-dollar box of chocolates ended up costing us a lot more.

So, after all the Pixie drama, we settled into a happy family of five.

Andrew, Pupa, Bronte, Pixie, and me. Pixie wanted to be the top dog, and Pupa would not let her. Bronte was the go-between for Pupa and Pixie. Pixie kept getting her massages and getting better and better. Soon, her trauma was gone, and she felt safe.

Pixie taught Bronte how to get out of the puppy fence we put in the family room. Once Bronte mastered the escape, we could not stop her. Bronte saw it as a puzzle and not a way of being naughty. Instead of the three dogs having the family room to stay in when Andrew and I went out at night, they all remained in the crate. Andrew snaps his fingers near the crate's entrance, and they all walk in.

Pixie is a bit of a chubby dog, so she got the nickname 'Fat Piggy.' Pixie likes to rub her back on the concrete or rug and make pig noises. She is a funny dog who also gets the name 'Troll Doggy.' Pixie likes to lay under the bed. When we play ball with Pupa and Bronte, after a few throws of the ball and them jumping on and off the bed, Pixie comes out barking and scares us all. Pupa and Bronte are frightened of Pixie, so they find their place on the bed, which is game over. Pixie does not like Pupa and Bronte playing chasings, either. She emerges from wherever she is, barking at them, and they stop playing.

Usually, dogs like to please their owners, and cats like to be pleased by their owners. Pixie had the name 'Cat-Dog,' as she loved sitting in the sun and wanted to be pleased by us.

Bronte loves playing ball. She has one particular ball that she plays with. We bought the same ball as a backup and thought introducing it in case the other ball broke or went missing would be a good idea. We introduced it too late as Bronte chased after it, saw it was the newer one, and walked away without picking it up. The original ball is still going.

One day, when Pupa was about eleven years old, she walked around in my office and started falling to the side until she fell over. We were concerned. I thought Pupa had a stroke. Pupa had developed a heart condition; a valve in her heart closes and does not open in time, so Pupa faints.

While I was in the hospital in September 2021, Andrew took both Pupa and Bronte for a walk, and Pupa fainted again. Andrew carried Pupa home. Pupa was taken to the vet and put on heart medication. After I got home from the hospital, Pupa's condition kept deteriorating. Her breathing became very difficult. Pupa would go to greet people at the door, faint and defecate. It was so sad. About six months later, in May 2022, we let Pupa go to heaven to be with Nannu. Before she went, we gave her some chocolate to try. Pupa liked it. We had Pupa cremated, and she sits in a nice wooden box on our television cabinet. Her plaque reads 'Our Faithful Pupa.' Inside Pupa's box with her ashes are the socks she had loved wearing when she had itchy feet. Her socks would calm her down and let her rest.

We did not realise how much stress and worry we were carrying around with Pupa being so sick. It was a relief to let Pupa go and not be so sad and worried about her. We took Bronte with us to say goodbye to Pupa. When Pupa was dead,

Bronte knew as she turned her back on her.

I spent a few days chatting with Bronte about Pupa, ensuring she was all okay. I probably did it more for myself than Bronte.

Then we had two dogs. Bronte and Pixie. Things were a lot calmer for a while. The house dynamics changed a bit as Bronte and Pixie did not make any fuss over who was at the door. Life was tranquil.

In December 2021, Pixie was no longer Fat Piggy. Pixie lost quite a bit of weight. Bronte started fighting with Pixie a lot, and we started getting a bit concerned that Bronte would hurt Pixie. We took Pixie to the vet in January 2023 and discovered she had lost half a kilo in a month. This was too much weight for such a small dog. Camille discussed with us that there was something seriously wrong with Pixie. We could do expensive tests to prove this, but the result would still be to let her go to heaven with Nannu and Pupa. Pixie was fifteen years old. Like Pupa, Pixie was cremated and sits in a nice wooden box on our television cabinet. Pixie's plaque reads, "Pixie 'Piggy' Doggie." A stuffed toy banana is in Pixie's box, along with her ashes. We thought that it was a good representation of all the fruit Pixie loved to eat. Her favourite fruit was a banana.

Currently, we still have Bronte with us. A month after Pixie passed away, we looked after a little dog named Watson. Bronte was not interested in having another dog in the house as a fourteen-year-old dog. Bronte is happy to be on her own with us. Bronte does not ask for much; she has a Schmacko in the morning and behaves like a four-year-old puppy until she gets one. She runs around, wagging her tail, jumping up and down off the furniture. After getting her treat, Bronte instantly becomes an old fourteen-year-old dog, slowly walking around, going in and out of the house into the backyard several times a day, and sleeping. Life is pretty quiet. I think we are saving up all of our tears of grief for when Bronte dies; then we will feel the loss of all three of our dogs.

In Pursuit...

- Andrew and I are privileged to have had the three dogs. They all love in their own unique way. We lived in harmony together. The dogs were our substitute children.

- A dog is man's best friend.

Pupa

Bronte

Pixie

PART 3

LIFE'S REFLECTIONS

Chapter 11
My Faith

From the time I can remember, my family always told me that God wanted me here for a reason. I have heard this my whole life.

My difficult entry into the world, the lack of oxygen, and the brain damage causing cerebral palsy made me different.

My 'difference' makes me stand out. In some ways, this has made me unforgettable or inspirational. I have not just blended in or faded into the background, even though, at times, I wish that I could have.

I would have given anything to be 'normal.' Instead, I learned to fit in by being good at things and excelling at others.

I always believed in God and prayed and spoke to God. My parents were Catholic, so their everyday language has God in it.

My determination is something that I know is God-given. I was determined to be like my sisters from an early age, even though they were much older than me. My sisters were the people I aspired to be like. I know Mum worked hard to help me achieve my physical goals. I started talking at nine months, and a relative also told me that my parents spoke to me like an understanding adult.

When I was four years old, I was napping at my Nanna's house in Malta, and Mum was next door having a cup of tea. I woke up and called my Mum, but she was not there. I got onto the floor, crawled down twenty-seven stairs, opened the door, sat on the edge of the door ledge, pulled the door closed behind me, and crawled onto the footpath, which was very rough. I crawled up the neighbour's five steps and called out to Mum as I could not open their front gate to get to the front door. Mum and the neighbour heard me calling out and came running. The neighbour exclaimed, "Wow, she has willpower!" I could have sat in bed crying and being scared that my Mum was not there. Instead, I chose to take action.

My nanna was a devout Catholic. In Malta, Nanna walked to her local church every morning. There was a particular church that she loved. It was the Church of the Redeemer. Nanna taught all her grandchildren a prayer. I was taught this prayer when I was five or six. As I grew up, Nanna sent me other prayers that she would get from the church in English through the mail. Nanna prayed for us every day. At Nanna's wake, my cousins and I gathered and said the prayer Nanna had taught us when we were young. Nanna was our family's spiritual warrior.

This is the Maltese prayer I was taught translated into English:

Maltese	English
Mulejja ha norqod,	Lord, I am going off to sleep
Ma-nafs x'se jkun fija	I do not know what's in store for me
Nirikmanda ruhi l-Alla	I offer my soul to the Lord
Il Virgini Maria	And to the Virgin Mary.
Viva Gesu	Praise, Jesus
Viva Maria	Praise, Mary
San Gusep itlob ghalina	Saint Joseph, pray for me.
Bezzjani Mummy	Bless me, Mummy
Bezzjani Daddy	Bless me, Daddy
Bezzjani Nanna	Bless me, Nanna
Bezzjani kulhad	Bless me, everyone.
Santa Rita fejjqni	Saint Rita, heal me
Fejjqni kulhad	Heal me, everyone!

I recently learned from my cousin, Maria, that the Maltese prayer Nanna taught us was for me to be healed so I could go live in Malta with them. That makes me feel teary and emotional. Forty-five years later, Maria and I are still praying that prayer.

I remember attending scripture class when I was in a special school. Our teacher was Mrs Philips, and her son, Mark, was in my class. Mrs Philips was very kind and gentle, showing God's love and gentleness in the way she taught us.

When I started public school in year five, I made friends with Susan, who is still my friend today. We probably hung out more when I was in year six and throughout high school and beyond. Susan has always been a Christian example to me and a great role model. As adults, we visited Koorong, the Christian bookshop, which was always a highlight. I would always buy a book or two and read them.

When I was still in primary school, I participated in my Holy Communion. A nun would come to my house and teach me. I do not remember much about what she taught me, but she introduced me to retractable crayons. I fell in love with them, and as a fifty-year-old, I have a pack that I use from time to time.

In high school, I attended the lunchtime scripture group. I think I mainly attended because my friends did; it was a safe place, and we were inside instead of standing around outside like cattle.

When I was twenty-one, my cousin, Scott, committed suicide, and my whole world turned upside down. On the surface, I could not understand how such a healthy, popular young man with everything going for him would choose to end his life. I know that many suicides are because of mental health issues, and more awareness is coming to light now.

At the time, however, I could not help comparing my life to Scott's. He was fit and healthy. I was in a wheelchair. He had lots of friends. I had a few. He was getting engaged. I had not even had my first kiss. He worked. I had never had a job. I felt guilty that a healthy person, with a lot going for him, would be dead, and I, a person with a disability and not much going for me, would still be alive.

I was angry at God for taking Scott and leaving me here on earth. I guess this was my introduction to adulthood. Life does not always make sense in the eyes of humans. God has a bigger and better plan.

When I was twenty-four, I received my Confirmation. I led the class at my place. With the help of some knowledgeable parents in the group, I learnt a lot, and I hope the children did too.

I asked my best friend, Susan, to be my sponsor, and the name I chose for the confirmation was Rebekah. It is customary to add a saint's name at your confirmation to aspire to and look up to.

I always had this feeling that I would marry a Christian man. When I was twenty-five, I met Andrew. He invited me to attend church with him. I enjoyed the teaching as it was pretty academic and thought-provoking. Andrew bought me a bible to read, and I read it cover to cover, asking questions along the way. It was the first time I had read the bible through.

As I was brought up Catholic, there was a bit of friction because Andrew felt that Protestants had a purer faith. We had a few arguments over the fact that I thought Andrew was putting my Catholic faith down, and I was angry at this. One argument ended with my saying, "Fine! I'll believe what you believe!" Andrew responded, "No, I want you to have your own faith."

The journey of discovering what it meant to be an honest Christian continued, and one day in church, the Holy Spirit came upon me, and I started to cry. It was a feeling of release and submission all at the same time.

At the time, we went to a church in Baulkham Hills and were married under the church auspice. A year after we married, we moved to a church closer to our home. Our new church was more welcoming and accommodating to my physical needs. The church sermons at our new church were more practical.

I did a lot of my learning about God and the Bible by researching studies I could get from the internet. We were also in a Bible study that fed us.

As a newly married couple, we regularly did devotionals in the morning.

I enrolled to do some vigorous online learning of the Bible. I only completed one unit, but it was very impactful.

I would later teach a similar subject at a certificate three level at Fusion.

All I learned about God as a new Christian up to this point was theoretical. I was around twenty-nine and thought that if I was 'good,' life would be easy, and I could have everything I prayed for.

I was not ready for what God had in store for me to make me the Warrior Princess I am today.

I remember sharing with my Bible study group as I was going into my thirtieth year that I had never felt happier or more at peace with my life than I had felt at that moment.

And then...

I tried to have a baby, and nothing was happening. When I got the news that we could not conceive naturally, I could not believe that God would allow me to get married but not allow me to have children. What? Why?

I prayed a lot while I went through IVF, and each cycle was a "No" from God. I asked God, "When will it be my turn to get a 'yes,' Lord?"

One particular cycle was the hardest; towards the end of a cycle, my sister-in-law told me that she had fallen pregnant accidentally, and then a day or two later, I discovered I was not pregnant.

I was furious at God, and I yelled and screamed and pretty much threw a big tantrum. I finally surrendered, as I had nothing left. Then, another level of spiritual maturity kicked in, and I stopped holding onto God — as I thought I had to. God started holding onto me. I felt a shift where I was no longer in control of my spiritual and somewhat emotional safety. God was keeping me safe, and I just had to lean into Him and let Him.

After this, I calmed down, lay in God's arms, and rested.

Sometimes, I gave God the silent treatment because I was so angry at Him. Guess who won that game? Not me.

I learned that God is not precious, and I will not hurt His feelings. We can yell at Him, and after we get it all out of our system, God will wrap His arms around us like the best, most perfect father in the world. He catches our tears in jars. I think He has had to find a bucket for mine.

The training God gave me while trying to get pregnant is something I would not have gotten any other way. I believe that through our hardships, we learn the best. We may not see what we are learning there and then, but months and years later, we will see it.

Nothing we go through is ever wasted. It can give us compassion and insight to help others. It can prepare us for what is to come later in life.

A beautiful lady at church gave me a framed quote from the Bible. It says:

"For I know the plans I have for you," declares the Lord, "plans to prosper you and not to harm you, plans to give you hope and a future." Jeremiah 11:29 (NIV).

When I took a break from trying to conceive, Andrew and I started volunteering at Fusion.

Fusion is a Christian international youth and community organisation. It helps communities to knit together and look after their youth by running various programs.

My being at Fusion was a big learning curve for everyone. I worked in the Western Sydney campus. The morning tea room was upstairs. I was fit enough to climb the stairs often and have someone bring up my chair. Morning tea was a time for having a cuppa, food, and, most importantly, a Bible study

— a short life story tied to scripture and prayer.

God taught me that nothing was impossible with Him.

I did various jobs in the organisation, which always exceeded the expectations of the team leader for whom I worked. I did some training with Fusion and part of the course involved going to Uluru with at-risk kids. I wanted to go with the other students. The team leader was against it. I showed that it was doable, and off we went. Andrew and I managed two weeks getting on and off a bus, camping, and doing everything the other students did. It was one of the best times I have ever had. I was exhausted when I got home, but I was so satisfied.

After finishing the training, I was asked to run the course. It was a significant role, but God prepared me by giving me bigger and bigger responsibilities within Fusion. After doing this role, I knew I could take on any other role. God knows what He is doing, even in the area of work.

God always says to me, "I've got this, Martha. All in my time. My timing is perfect in every area of your life. Just trust me."

There have been times when God has used me to speak to a group at church and, afterwards, people have said that the message could have only come from me because I was not like everybody else. I am not someone that people compare themselves to. Not being 'normal' comes in handy sometimes.

Dad passed away in mid-2015. Before Dad passed away, he gave me some words of wisdom I think I will keep remembering until the day I die. I had been struggling with an infection, and I was on some pretty heavy medication to clear it. I went to visit Mum and Dad, and I told Dad that I felt like I was suffering. Dad's reply to me was, "Christ suffered more." These three words helped me shift my focus and be strong. I knew I could withstand the pain and discomfort of what I was going through because of what Christ did for me.

Dad was sick for three weeks before he passed away. There were two unique visits I had with Dad before his death. I feel very privileged to have had these times.

DAD'S LAST MEAL

I went in to visit with Dad in his ICU room.

I found him sitting up in bed, eating with all his heart!

As he ate his mashed potato, he told me how good it tasted!

He had not eaten anything in weeks besides his sister Georgina's soup.

He continued eating some beans.

Then, he was having trouble picking up his meat with his fork.

I offered that Andrew could cut it up for him.

Dad replied, "No, it's okay," as he picked up the meat, gravy and all, with his fingers and took a small bite!

Dad tried to give me his ice cream to eat, but I refused and suggested he eat it with his jelly.

He kept telling me how good the food tasted as he smeared mashed potato and gravy on his oxygen pipe that was attached to his nose and ran down the side of his face on the way to his mouth.

I just loved watching him eat and enjoying it so much!

I left his ICU room, not knowing that he was never going to be alert again.

But my heart was full of joy and pleasure watching Dad eat his last meal with all his heart.

The ice cream he offered me was eaten by Mum, who did not refuse the offer.

There they sat, Mum eating the ice cream and Dad eating the jelly, together.

Martha

THE LAST KISS GOODBYE

On my last visit with Dad, I decided to kiss him.

Dad's nurse lowered his bed, and I aligned my wheelchair with Dad's head.

I gently stood up and bent my torso to kiss Dad's cheek.

I prayed for 'no twitches' and none were around — phew!

I kissed Dad on the cheek, then I lowered my cheek to Dad's lips, and he kissed me back!

Our last kiss goodbye — until we meet again.

Martha xxx

I had to have an operation to remove my deep brain stimulation battery and lead three days before Dad passed away. Somehow, God gave me the strength to leave the hospital after Dad passed away and be with my family to prepare and direct Dad's funeral.

I was not angry at God for taking Dad. It was Dad's time to go. I missed Dad a lot and was furious that he was not around to answer my questions and solve my carpentry problems. As a family, we talk about Dad every day. Primarily, how he would respond to what we were saying and doing: it is fun!

I think that my DNA changed when Dad passed away. A piece of him became a piece of me. Perhaps DNA becomes dominant or active. I saw it when Dad's Dad passed away. Is it the way past generations live on?

We now have a little human; my brother's daughter, Amelia Jane Farrugia, was born six years after Dad passed away. My beautiful niece, Amelia, has her grandfather's initials and is always told about her grandfather. Amelia is a delightful, funny little girl we all love. I believe that God gave us Amelia as a gift. She will resemble a lot of Dad as she gets older.

Being in a coma two years ago due to a hip operation going wrong had me look at my relationship with God again.

As I was sleeping, I had some bizarre hallucinations to do with death. One thing I was told in my hallucinogenic state is that you do not take anything with you when you die. Of course, we know about the material things. I was told that it also includes the education we get on Earth and our position in the world. None of this is taken with us when we die. It is all just stripped away.

So why are we striving to achieve? What if we aim to live for God? To do His work and follow Him? Go into the world and share the Good News?

As well as being told I would not take anything with me when I die, I felt like I was floating in space on a journey somewhere. The space was dark, and I was heading somewhere, but I never got there. I wonder if I was journeying towards heaven — not actually there. It was peaceful and pleasant but dark. There were no shining, bright lights.

I spent some time discussing this journey with our Pastor and Bible study group because I kept feeling sick when people in the church spoke about how they would see bright lights when they went to heaven. I asked myself, "What must I do to go to heaven? Have I got it all wrong?"

The conclusion my Pastor and I came to is that it may have been just a journey or a journey towards, but I was not anywhere near death. I am okay with this answer for now.

When I woke up from my coma, there was a thickness in the air. This thickness, I believe, was a spirit of prayer that surrounded me. I felt this tangible cloud of air in the rooms I was in — in the ICU ward and especially in the west ward.

As I got better, Andrew explained that he had hacked into my Facebook account, and he and my niece, Leeanne, had periodically updated my contacts with what was going on with my health. Many of my contacts prayed for me, so I had this air of prayer surrounding me. What a privilege to have felt and experienced that.

At the beginning of my recovery, I asked, "Why did I survive?" I do not feel like I have anything to offer this world. And I do not have any children to raise. I concluded that I needed to keep going and get better. The peaceful phrase God gave me is, "It is what it is," and more recently, "I've got this."

Recently, I wanted to strip away the 'noise' around God and find the pure God for myself. I saw God while in the ocean on a cruise in a sorry state. I was worn out, tired, and depressed. I asked God to help me, and He said, "Here I am. I'm waiting for you to ask." I asked God to help me find peace and balance, and my inner struggle subsided. Overnight, I was made whole again.

I do not know what God wants me to do, but I will keep being determined to be better in God's strength and encourage those around me.

I want to represent a beacon of hope to others and show that nothing is impossible. With God, walls can be broken down and, as prisoners of life, we can be free. We may not always get what we want, but we get what we need and what is good for us.

We have to stop trying to do for people and be for God. As it is written in Psalm 46:10, "Be still and know that I am God..." (NIV)

In Pursuit...

- I cannot imagine not having God to discuss things in my life.

- God is the only one who knows more and knows best.

- No human knows what God knows.

- With God, life is possible!

Chapter 12

Holidays and Adventures

I am a Bit of a Thrill-Seeker — I Like Fast and Dangerous

I have been fortunate to go on many holidays and adventures in my fifty years. Where people used to go camping or caravanning for holidays, my parents took me overseas to Malta.

One of my favourite trips was with my Dad in 1984. I was eleven years old, and all my cousins in Malta were on school holidays. My cousins and I are around the same age. My Nannu hired a car for my Dad, and he would take all five of us cousins around Malta, buying us ice-creams and sightseeing. We all had the best time together.

My cousins, Lorenza, Jeanette, Maria, Paul, and I had the best summer that year. We were all great friends, and I remember the laughter and us joking around together, which gave a great vibe.

My cousins all lived within walking distance of Nanna and Nannu's place, so Dad would tell them to meet us there at a particular time. We would all jump in the car and go.

The most memorable parts were that Dad would tie my wheelchair onto the roof racks, and four of us would sit crammed into the back of this tiny yellow Fiat while Dad drove and my cousin Paul would sit shotgun.

Otherwise, Mum encouraged me to go on holidays and camps that I was invited to go on by The Crippled Children's Society. My social worker would arrange for me to go. Mrs Hackette was such a lovely older lady with grey hair. She was gentle, kind, and caring. Her role was to support my parents in bringing me up with any assistance they needed. She listened to my Mum, helped Dad get an interest-free loan to renovate our home to be more wheelchair accessible, and assisted me in going to camps.

The camps I went on were sport and recreation camps at Point Wolstencroft. Teenagers with disabilities would go together with older teenagers studying at university to gain experience in their field of study, such as occupational therapists, physiotherapists, and sports scientists. The teenagers were our support workers.

The first year I went, there was one-on-one support. The girl supporting me was a bit bossy, and I had to tell her to stop as she was bossing me around a lot more than my parents ever did.

The camps had other families attend, and we would do sports, canoeing and sailing, archery, or swimming during the day, and in the evening, we would have activities in the main hall. It was always lots of fun and laughter.

The second year I went to the camp, there were many more children — about six — and only two support workers. The support workers were very busy and did not have time to shower. I ended up offering to help in any way I could. One boy needed constant supervision but was happy to play table tennis, so I would sit with him while the support worker took a shower. The other support worker would take the four other children to the morning activity.

A few sports science university students at the camp were interested in helping us out, so the load was shared again. One student, Mel, became my pen pal, and we wrote to each other for many years. Mel went on to do the camps with children with disabilities for a few years.

I enjoyed sailing, and setting up the jib would be my job. One day, we went sailing on a very windy day. The boat overturned, and I got dragged under as my legs were tangled in the ropes. All I could hear underwater was the water gurgling, and I could see ropes everywhere. Everything was in slow motion, and I wondered if I would ever find the surface and AIR! Fortunately, I found an air pocket and could call for help. Someone came and dragged me down and out. They had forgotten that I was with them. It was a terrifying experience, and my life flashed past me, in colour. I loved sailing, but after that experience, I was hesitant to go sailing again.

Another fantastic adventure I got to go on with camps for disabled children was caving at Jenolan Caves. We put headlamps on and crawled through the caves. The caves were cool, silty, and muddy, but it was a fantastic experience, and I was with many funny children.

We all crawled into a cave and stopped in an opening. We were told stories about how the workers worked in the caves with candles. We lit some candles and turned off our headlamps to see what that looked and felt like.

There was a blind boy in our group, and his mate decided to guide his finger towards the candle and the blind boy burnt his finger and snuffed out the candle. You could hear the blind boy say, "Ah, you idiot," and his friend laughing. These are the pranks of disabled children.

As a teenager, I also got to go water skiing with family friends who had a speedboat. I would sit in an inflatable tube and water ski behind the boat. I loved it and could never get enough.

Before I started university, I went on a holiday with my best friend, Susan, whom I knew from primary school. We went to South Molle Island in 1996. South Molle is an island off the coast of North Queensland. To get there, you have to travel by plane and boat. It was the most fun holiday ever. We made friends with three other couples. Each day, happy hour went on for four hours. The barman would put together concoctions that we just had to test. The eight of us would rock up to the restaurant and ask to sit together, only to be turned away and told to come back in an hour when they would have a table ready for us, so to fill in the time, we drank more.

One night, we were sitting at the edge of the pool and one guy, Marty, told a joke that I thought was hilarious, and I fell face-first in the pool. The joke was, "How do you like your eggs in the morning? 'Unfertilised.'" When I first met Marty, he asked, "Do you want any bread?" I replied, "No, I've had breakfast." Marty was offering me bread to feed the fish! The shenanigans we got up to on that holiday were hilarious!

I went on many holidays with Susan, to her parents' holiday home and on several trips to where Susan had job interviews. I was Susan's wing-woman until she found her school.

Another activity I have enjoyed is 'iFly,' where you are suspended in the air by air blowing up under you. It is much like skydiving, but you go up instead of down. To iFly, you must wear a suit, goggles, earplugs, and a helmet. The suits have handles, and two instructors grab the handles on each side of my body, left and right, take me into the wind chamber, and fly me around. I love the feeling of being suspended in the air. Moving your arms and legs in specific directions and the suit structure means the air can take you up or bring you down.

I have had this bucket list since high school, and I do not want to add anything to it until I have ticked these three things off. The three things are: One, ride in the sidecar of a motorbike; Two, skydive out of an aeroplane; and Three, meet Neil Finn from Crowded House.

Out of the three things on my bucket list, I can say that I have ticked one thing off.

I have ridden in the sidecar of a motorbike. Kevin, a friend of the family, is into bikes in a big way. He has half a dozen bikes. One of his bikes is a Triumph. Kevin had a sidecar made for the bike. The sidecar is comfortable. However, when you are driving around in it, you realise how close to the ground you are sitting, and seeing the road pass by takes some getting used to. At first, I felt sick from the realisation, but halfway through the ride, I was used to it all and enjoyed it. I wore my fake leather jacket and boots and my black pants. Kevin provided the helmet, and I was set to go. I loved that experience.

Another two experiences I got to have were snow skiing and surfing thanks to my fantastic friend Gretta, who also has cerebral palsy. I met Gretta at the shops. One week, I passed her and smiled. The following week, I stopped and chatted with her. We became Facebook friends and talked a lot via Messenger. Gretta is always doing adventurous things and blogging about it. You can find Gretta's blogs here: www.onourowntracks.com. I am proud to say that I introduced Gretta to iFly!

Gretta goes snow skiing every year, and she set me up with the right contacts to book accommodation, ski passes, and a ski chair and driver. Another friend, Kate, from church, instructed me on clothing I needed. As the snow skiing season was nearing its end, everything I needed to buy was half-price or less. I got a ski helmet, goggles, snow pants, gloves, and boots. Kate instructed me to get undergarments I could use daily, like leggings and long-sleeved T-shirts.

I went with Gretta, two of her support workers, and Andrew.

We had two days of skiing. I was sitting in this very technical seat and fully strapped in — torso, legs, arms. My ski instructor/driver, Ursina, from Switzerland, was incredible. She taught me how to lean into turns. I was even loaded onto a chair lift and pushed off the ski lift once we reached the top. To access the chair lifts, you must go through a boom gate. To do this, you have a paid ski pass in the arm of your jacket in a zipped pocket that you swipe to have the boom gate open

— being on a chair lift that goes up and up is fantastic. Ursina shared that I was spoiled by such great weather on my ski trip: big, bright blue skies, no snow or rain falling — crisp, perfect days.

The adrenaline rush as we went down the slopes was incredible. Such exhilaration! On the first half day, we took it a lot easier as I learned to feel my way and get used to the feeling of skiing. On the second half day, Ursina took me up higher, and we just skied all day, cutting up the corduroy snow that had not been skied on since the runs had been groomed the night before. We skied from Perisher to Mount Bulla.

Two half days of skiing was enough adrenaline for me. I wanted to go back again in the following years, but COVID hit, and rehabbing out of my coma has stopped me from going skiing again, but I hope to go again one day.

After skiing for the day, we would go out for lunch, return to the cabin, and go out for dinner. Pete Murray was playing a concert in the hall where we were staying, so Gretta, her support worker, Andrew, and I went to see him perform. Pete Murray is great in concert. We even got to meet him afterwards and he signed our CDs.

Gretta also shared with me that she had been surfing in Byron Bay with Emma from Ability Surf — www.abilitysurf. com.au — who had come up with a way for people with disabilities to experience surfing. I contacted Emma and arranged to meet her and go surfing.

Byron Bay is about ten hours north of where we live, so Andrew and I planned a road trip to catch up with people. Our first stop was Susan's in Tamworth, where we stayed for one night and caught up with Susan and Skye for dinner. Skye is another friend from primary school that Susan and I went to school with. On our way to Susan's, we stopped at Scone and ate scones at Crowded House Café!!! Susan had set up a lovely room for us to sleep in, but it was hot, so we slept on the lounge under the air conditioner. In the morning, we woke up, got ready, and hit the road again after breakfast. We then went via Eden, caught up with a friend, and went to Byron.

Byron has beautiful beaches, boutique places to stay, and places to eat, but the streets and paths need work. Byron Bay is a relaxed hippie town, and many people work to make ends meet so they can surf. There is a very eclectic vibe there.

We stayed at this little boutique accommodation, sharing the entertainment and kitchen space. The owner also lived onsite and had a dog that we just loved. We met a lovely French couple who resided in China and enjoyed time with them on their holiday.

Back to surfing: I met with Emma online before I left home so she could learn about my disability and ask me questions about my needs. Emma is a qualified occupational therapist who loves to surf. Emma thought it would be great to marry the two and teach people with disabilities to surf as a form of exercise and experience surfing. I went to just surf.

The big day finally came, and we met Emma at the beach. Emma was there with two volunteers to assist us. Emma asked me to wear an Ability Surf rashie, a life jacket, and my bike shorts. I was set. Emma produced a sand wheelchair from her Kombi van for me to sit on so they could drive me down to the water. Once we got to the water, we tried several positions on the surfboard. The surfboard is partially inflatable, making it more stable in the water.

I could sit on the surfboard and hold on to the handles of the board. Emma and her assistants would paddle me out to sea, catch a wave, and I would surf back into shore. They did that with me over and over again for an hour. I asked many questions about the surf and how they know which waves will roll into it. It is a great science that requires lots of practice and instinct. It was another adrenaline-filled afternoon with another sport I got to have a go at.

Since surfing, we have had COVID, and then I was in ICU, so no more crazy adventures have been had.

I will always be on the lookout for things, though — just because I am fifty does not mean I will stop!

I booked our first holiday after we were married, which surprised Andrew. We went on many holidays to the Gold Coast over the years. We tried finding the first place we stayed at many years later, but it had been redeveloped into a mega building.

One place we loved staying at is The Watermark. It is comfortable and has an inviting sitting area. We went to the theme parks on the Gold Coast and saw where Big Brother's first year was filmed. There were many televisions set up to see what each camera was filming. We also liked going to the outlet stores and accessing their wheelchair accessible buses or walking through the main street, Caval Avenue.

Kangaroo Island, off South Australia by ferry, is a holiday we both loved — once we sorted out the accommodation. A place we booked said they had wheelchair accessible accommodation, but when we saw it, it was not, so I looked for another place. The only problem was that the new accommodation was booked out for our last night, as Kangaroo Island was having a big festival, so we went back to South Australia one day early and stayed there a night and went straight to the airport as it was a scorching forty degrees Celsius; we got an earlier flight and came home.

Staying on Kangaroo Island was like stepping into the seventies. Everyone was laid back and friendly. We found a colourful Mexican restaurant that we loved eating at. Towards the end of our time on Kangaroo Island, we ate breakfast, lunch, and dinner there!

We travelled to Cairns, which felt relatively poor the year we went. The place we stayed at was a bargain; it was something like two hundred and fifty dollars for the week! The pool there was terrific, though. I would park myself on a deck chair, get onto the floor, and scoot to the water to cool down.

Airlie Beach was another throwback to the seventies. It

had healthy, alternative food options, was relaxed, and made you feel safe.

Another time, we travelled to Tasmania and stayed in Dutch-looking accommodation. We had to put our electric blankets on in January as it was cold — January is the middle of our summer.

We went to a seahorse farm, a lavender farm, and a strawberry farm. We also saw a model display that this man had set up in part of his home. When we got there, his wife shared that her husband had passed away a few months before. We were happy to leave, but she wanted to open the display and let us look around. She shared stories about her husband, which was a cathartic experience. We were willing to pay the entry fee, but she would not allow us.

Andrew and I have travelled to Melbourne several times to visit Andrew's uncle, aunt, and cousins. We usually travel by car. It is an eight-hour journey south. We stop at another aunt and uncle along the way, and cousins always call in for a visit. It is always a fun time of laughter and lots of good food. We explore the Melbourne CBD and visit a Café in the Daintree National Park. We think Melbourne is slower-paced than Sydney, but that may be because we are on holiday.

Melbourne's weather is not very kind to me, though. I often return home with a chest infection, so we limit our Melbourne holidays.

In the past five years, we have done heaps of cruises. Andrew and I love cruising. It is the easiest way for us to go on holiday. An entire city on a floating ship. Fully wheelchair accessible, food on hand whenever you are hungry. No need to hail a taxi or drive to get anywhere. Entertainment is everywhere, as well as social interaction or just some quiet time relaxing.

Our favourite ships are Princess, Carnival, and P&O. We like to leave from the Sydney cruise terminal so that I can take my power wheelchair and get myself around. The Sydney terminal is only an hour from where we live, so it works efficiently.

I like watching the ocean, with a breeze blowing my way, and reading. I am happy to chat, laugh, and maybe go to a show or gig. A bit of shopping might take place too.

Going onto shore may or may not happen, depending on whether they are docked or using tenders. If the ship is docked to the shore, I can get my chair down but not get on a tender as stairs are involved. Some islands or places that you dock may not be very wheelchair accessible either.

My mindset is that I will go on the cruise to enjoy it. If I get off onto shore to explore, it is a bonus. This way, I do not set myself up for any disappointment or get too stressed and tired.

My niece also introduced me to Belmont Caravan Park, which has entirely accessible villas. The place is on an inlet up north and is very picturesque. There are ducks, pelicans, and swans to watch. There are sailing boats out in the distance. The park is dog friendly, but unfortunately, no dogs are allowed in the villa.

I love talking to the dogs that I pass walking along the track. It is a gorgeous spot to stay. We have learned to take our food as restaurants and cafes are getting expensive, and it reduces the stress of finding somewhere to eat. A coffee van comes into the park, and we like getting daily coffee and hot chocolate to support local businesses.

In Pursuit...

- Holiday when you can and make memories. Who knows how long you will be healthy?

- Life is hard — play harder.

Getting ready to go for a ride in the
sidecar of a Triumph motorbike

iFly upside down

Getting ready to get on a ski lift with Ursina,
my ski driver

Surfing with Emma from Ability Surf

Chapter 13
That's Entertainment

A Tenant in a Crowded House watching two TVs

My whole life has been filled with music. My Dad loved music so much that he sang every day, and my Mum enjoyed singing even though she did not know many of the words. My Dad's favourite artists were Frank Sinatra and The Beatles. Dad used to sing You Make Me Feel So Young by Frank Sinatra all the time. There is a line that sings, "Picking up all those forget me nots." Dad used to sing, "Picking up all those spaghetti peanuts." We sang "spaghetti peanuts" my whole life. What the heck are spaghetti peanuts??? Lol!

By the time I was born and old enough to understand what was happening, my sisters were teenagers, so there was more music in the house: ABBA, Daryl Braithwaite, Cliff Richard, Queen, Skyhooks, Dragon, and Fleetwood Mac. Ruth had the radio on constantly.

I grew up watching Young Talent Time with my family. Our favourites were Tina Arena and John Bowles.

When I was nine or ten, my first album was Young Talent Time, and I still have it.

I also remember watching Countdown from a very early age. The presenter, Molly Meldrum, was always so passionate about music. Molly would always say, "Do yourself a favour and go out and get yourself..." whatever record/tickets to a concert he was plugging.

My very first concert at the Entertainment Centre was Culture Club in 1984.

My sister's friend, Judy, wrote to one of the newspapers and told them how much I loved music and that I was in a wheelchair. The newspaper gave her passes to a meet and greet so she and I could meet Culture Club and be part of their media conference, as well as tickets to attend their concert.

When I met Boy George, I remember him having huge hands. George shook my hand and signed my jumper. He wrote, "2 Martha, From Boy George." Then John Moss, the drummer, asked me for a kiss, and I kissed him on the cheek. I also met Roy and Mickey, but George and John made a big impression.

The media conference was packed with reporters and cameramen. I somehow put my hand up and asked a question. The press conference was shown on Terry Willesee Tonight, and I was shown asking my question.

After the meet and greet and the press conference, my two sisters, Judy and I, went to a Chinese restaurant in Chinatown for dinner. It was the first time I had been to the city and Chinatown was mayhem with all its hustle and bustle. Esther and I then went to see Culture Club in concert. We had seats in around the fifth row from the stage. The concert was larger than life, with Boy George changing his outfits multiple times. The music was booming, and the whole concert was a big production. Boy George was so beautiful, with his meticulous makeup, gorgeous hair, and colourful clothes — I loved it all!!

That first concert experience left a big impression on me. It was a drug and I wanted more.

After Culture Club split, Judy introduced me to Crowded House. The first song I heard was Don't Dream It's Over. After hearing that song, I was hooked. I bought their self-titled album in Parramatta with Dad, and I was very excited when Dad played it for me on the record player. I was in awe of the whole record: the art Nick Seymour painted on the front cover, all the words to the songs on the inside cover, and the photography. I also bought the cassette tape so I could play it on my tape recorder independently in my room. What I love is Neil Finn's lyrics. He writes exquisite lyrics that take your mind to places you have never been. You can hear the same song twice and be taken to different locations in your mind. I love that. If I ever were to meet Neil Finn, I would say, "Thank you for writing the soundtrack for my life."

I loved watching Rage, Video Hits, and MTV. I loved seeing the Crowded House videos. Don't Dream will always be my favourite song, and I want it played at my funeral as they walk my casket out.

There was a local CD shop that I went to every week, and I became friends with the owners.

The shop would host bands in the shopping centre, and I would be invited upstairs to meet the bands. I met Indecent Obsession and talked to David Dixon for ages. I was obsessed with Indecent Obsession for a time.

I used to buy Smash Hits magazine when it came out and, on occasion, I used to buy Rolling Stone magazine. My favourite thing to do after I read the magazine from cover to cover is to cut out the pictures and interview information about Crowded House and stick them in a folder/scrapbook I put together. I love Crowded House so much that I joined the fan club for a couple of years. The fan club members were called 'Tenants.' I still have my scrapbooks. I try to throw them away, but I just cannot.

As a school project for English, I did my assignment on Crowded House. I lived and breathed everything Crowded House. Even an art project had me using the album cover as my inspiration.

I have been to seven Crowded House/Neil Finn concerts

My favourite was seeing Neil Finn with Jimmy Barnes at Angel Street Theatre with my friend, Amie. These seats were the best I had ever sat in!!! Fourth row from the front! It's a perfect gig! I wrote to the theatre to share how happy I was to sit near the front and that they had done a great job sitting me in the crowd.

To buy wheelchair seating tickets, you must ring and book through 'special bookings.' There is that 'special' word again. The allocated seats are not always the 'best' seats. Some venues are considering better seats, like Angel Street Theatre!

It is excellent to have allocated seats, but if I were not in a wheelchair, I would have more options.

My favourite venues are Angel Street Theatre and Selina's VIP lounge, although I imagine I would not be allowed up there anymore due to work, health, and safety issues.

You cannot go to concerts with more than one or two friends as you cannot sit together due to a limited number of wheelchair accessible seats and accompanying 'normal' seating.

Alongside my love for music, I love watching sports.

My first introduction to tennis was in high school when I was asked to keep score in physical education. Rachel, a girl in my class, patiently taught me how to score. Pat Cash was playing the year I started watching on TV and every summer for the last thirty-five years.

I have been to the Sydney International at White Bay, where I got hit with a tennis ball on the knee, but it was a soft hit. I have been to the Australian Open in Melbourne. Andre Agassi walked past us. I said, "Hi." He said, "Hi" and kept walking. Aunty Gemma and I went to Olympic Park to watch tennis when she came to Australia from Malta. As we are both tennis tragics we made sure we went to the tennis together. She came to Australia at the right time for us to go and we loved it.

I went to the 2000 Olympics to watch the athletics first heats of the one hundred metres, as my cousin, Sue, and my friend, Mario, represented Malta.

My cousin, Sue, was the second fastest in Malta. Sue ran the race of her life to beat the girl coming first and win a place on the team to go to the Sydney Olympics to see her Australian family.

Mario was always coming first in his races. When I met Mario in 1993, it was announced that Sydney, Australia, would be hosting the Olympics in 2000. I had said to Mario, "See you in Sydney, mate!" and I did!

A couple of years ago, Andrew and I became soccer fans and went to a lot of the home games of the Western Sydney Wanderers. We were members for two years, and I even got to march with the soccer fanatics! It was loud and fun.

Around thirteen years ago, the Big Bash League started in Australia. It is a twenty over per side cricket match that is very colourful and high energy. Our local team is the Sydney Thunder; its uniform is lime green, my favourite colour. Andrew and I went to see a double header where the women's Thunder team played the women's Brisbane Heat team. The men's teams then played their match. I was wearing my WBBL Thunder shirt that just came out.

The women's match was entertaining, and we loved watching it. Unfortunately, the men's match was washed out by rain. We got soaked but had lots of fun. We were given capes to wear, and I attached mine to my chair and drove around fast to have my cape fly out behind me. It was lots of fun. I was sharing my cape antics with a friend at church, and she told me my superpower was farting. I was laughing so hard I farted!

I have watched the BBL and the WBBL whenever they were on TV. The commentary is always hilarious, and the players put on a fantastic hit-fest. It is a fun show to watch in December and January. The most fun is the Adelaide Strikers match every New Year's Eve. It is always a spectacular show.

This year, we saw Australia play Pakistan in the Sydney pink test. We went to day two and it was slow. I found it relaxing and the weather was not too hot. We sat in the shade. Unfortunately, they stopped playing at 3pm because it became overcast, dark, and raining.

Andrew and I went to the cricket with some friends. We shared food and ate and drank all day. It was a relaxing day.

I find January tough as cricket and tennis are often on simultaneously, and I must choose what to watch. Every year, I ask Andrew for two TVs side by side so that I can watch both at the same time. Perhaps I need to devise a plan for two TVs that Andrew can execute.

I enjoy watching sports as much as I can while it is on because once February is here, all the tennis and cricket is usually over, and I am at a loss.

In Pursuit...

- Silence can seem so deafening. Music is the backdrop to my life.

- Sport is relaxing, stressful, and fun – a real time waster.

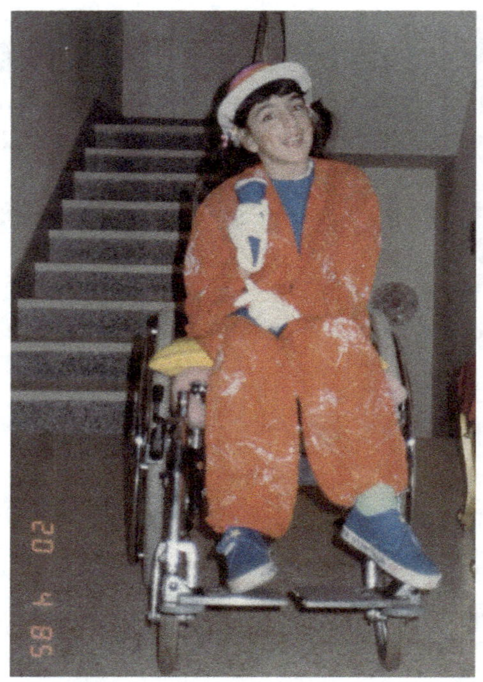

In my Boy George outfit made by Mum's Aunty Rose

With David Dixon from Indecent Obsession

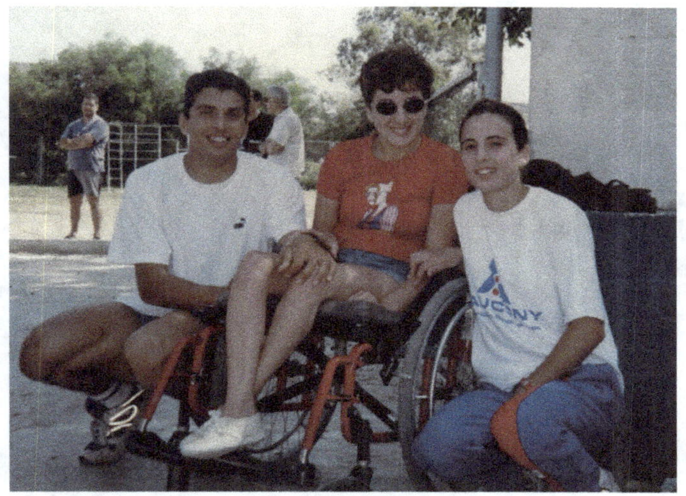

Mario, me, and my cousin, Sue, in 2000

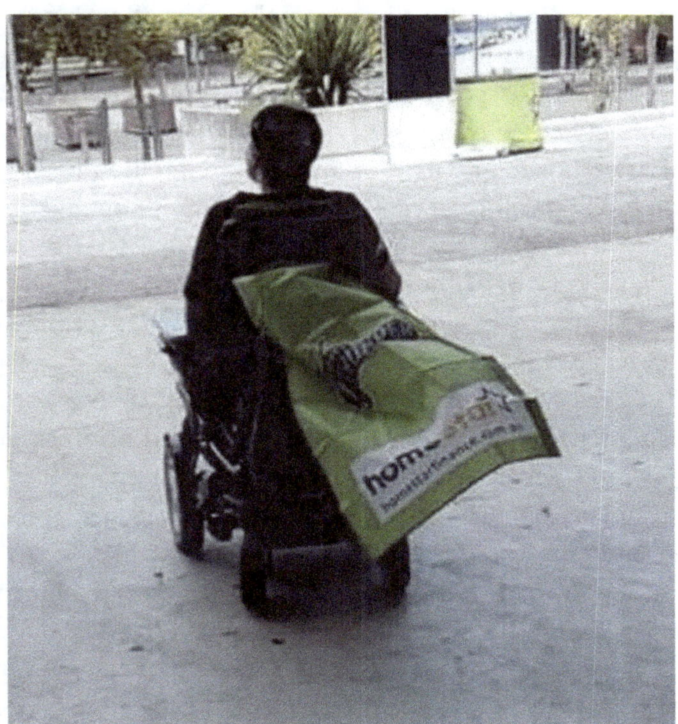

Me in my Thunder cape

Chapter 14
Medical Interventions

Mum was a realist. Her ideas regarding medical interventions were the best for me! "We accept Martha with her disability, and we will do the best we can to progress her as much as we can by reminding her to sit up straight, to swallow often, and not dribble. To encourage her to try and control her movements as much as possible." These were areas that my Mum instinctively knew to do.

If I was not in any pain or any life-threatening health situation, no medical interventions were going to be taken.

I saw a paediatrician every year until I was sixteen years old. Every year, he wondered why I could not walk. I do not think he knew much about cerebral palsy. Aside from my disability, he always saw me as healthy.

The area of concern I had for my whole life was asthma. Dad spent many early hours of the morning driving me to the hospital because I could not breathe. At five years old, you could buy a nebuliser at the chemist and get prescriptions for Ventolin and Intal to mix and put in the nebuliser to breathe it in. This saved my Dad a lot of early morning drives to Randwick Children's Hospital. At the age of fourteen, my asthma was under control with preventative puffers and relieving puffers. I still needed antibiotics if I got a cold, which would become a chest infection. Otherwise, I was a healthy child, adolescent, and adult.

I did have three operations while I was a child.

One operation was of no consequence to me in that I had my groin stretched to hopefully help my leg behave better when I was eight years old. The operation did nothing. I will later tell you why.

The operation was very disruptive to me and my family. After the operation, I was put in plaster on both legs from the top of my thigh to the top of my ankle, and I had a bar of wood between my knees, stretching my legs out in the shape of a triangle. Because of the shape, it was suggested that I stay in a home for children with disabilities in Beverly Hills for three and a half weeks while I was in plaster. The home had a school attached. The home was for unwanted children with disabilities. Their parents rarely or never visited their children. I did not do well in the home as an eight-year-old. My parents visited me every day and brought me food, but I could not eat because I was so distressed. The other children did not like that my parents visited me and cared about me so much. They were angry. After a week, my Dad said, "That's it, you're coming home with us!"

Dad turned me sideways to fit me through the car door of the back seat of the 'Green Limousine.' He sat me facing the window and drove me home. We did not wear seat belts in the back seat back then.

Once home, Dad put a board under the cushion of my wheelchair to support the wooden bar holding my legs, and I just had to tilt my legs a bit to get through the doorways. My hair was washed in the kitchen sink, and I was given sponge baths. I was happy to be home. When it came time to get the casts off my legs, a circular saw cut them in half. Once the casts were open, my left leg spasmed, and I pulled a muscle in my thigh. It was excruciating. It was decided that the pole would be removed, but the bottom half of the casts would be left on, and my legs would be wrapped in bandages to keep them straight. I then had to use hydrotherapy at school to learn to bend my legs again. Because the casts were heavy in the knee area, my right knee turned in, and that is how it remains now when I straighten my leg.

The other two operations were in my mouth. I somehow grew a benign tumour over my teeth on the left side of my mouth that needed to come out. A couple of years later, I had to get a bone and some teeth removed in preparation to get braces put on my teeth. I had buck teeth, and I desperately needed braces.

The rest of my childhood was without any medical intervention.

At the age of twenty-one, I developed a twitch that was causing me grief. I remember going to a specialist that treated epilepsy. I was filmed doing specific movements, and a board of specialists analysed the recordings to see how I could be helped. The outcome was that I was prescribed a drug to treat this twitch, but it could cause organ damage. I took the prescription home but I never filled it.

I had never taken drugs for my disability, as I lived happily without them.

When I was in my mid-thirties, I saw a new GP who asked if I saw any medical professional to deal with my disability. My response was, "No." My GP asked, "Are you interested in seeing a neurologist to see if there are any new medicines to make you more comfortable?" I was happy to make an appointment.

The specialist, Doctor Woods, was a kind gentleman who conducted many tests and then asked if I was interested in meeting with another neurologist at Nepean Hospital looking to conduct a trial on people with cerebral palsy. I said, "Yes!"

It took a while for the appointment to happen. I met Doctor Krause, and it was the funniest experience ever. Doctor Krause did an exhaustive number of tests, and after each test, he exclaimed, "This is unbelievable! I can't believe this is happening!" He behaved more like a mad scientist than a doctor. The reason for all the exclamations was because I have the purest form of dystonic cerebral palsy he had encountered, and the trial he was looking at conducting was to try deep brain stimulation on patients with dystonic cerebral palsy. Doctor Krause knew a lot about my particular cerebral palsy, like why I could not walk and why the operation on my groin made no difference to my body.

I could not walk due to the instability caused by the involuntary movements. There was no amount of practising walking that could eliminate involuntary movements. The only way the involuntary movements could stop was if changes were made in my brain.

The same was true when I had my groin stretched for my leg to behave — again, my brain needed to be altered.

Doctor Krause asked if I wanted to be part of a trial. By putting electrodes in the deep part of the brain called globus pallidus internus, signals are then pulsed through that part of the brain to bypass and eliminate the involuntary movements. I was happy to be a guinea pig and try. What did I have to lose?

I could not just say "Yes" and start the process.

First, I had to join a private health fund and wait one year for it to kick in. The medical procedure had to be done in the private hospital as it was not funded in the public system.

Second, a panel of medical professionals in the field was formed, and I had to go before the panel to be assessed. Once everyone approved me, another series of tests needed to be conducted to evaluate and approve my eligibility for the trial.

One of the tests I found to be harsh. I had a metal helmet on my head and wires placed on different limbs that then conducted what seemed like an electric shock, and my arm or leg reacted. I was not too fond of that test and was very angry about it. I passed, though; my body responded how the clinical team wanted it to.

I also did some psychological testing and was found to have a high IQ.

I then met the surgeon who was going to do the operation. I wrote him a note that said, "While you are working in my brain, can you please turn down my movements, turn up my intelligence, and you can leave my sense of humour as I am already funny enough!"

The next set of tests was recorded on video, and it was done again once I had the deep brain stimulation in, and it was working.

The tests included putting my hands out in front and touching my nose or shoulders, pouring water into cups, walking, and doing other things I had trouble doing.

I was asked a couple of days before the test if I could be filmed for a piece on Sunday Night, a television program. I agreed, so a camera crew and the presenter for my piece, Doctor John D'Arcy, were present at the test. I grew up watching Doctor John present on television; meeting him was an honour.

A couple of days before I was due to have the operation to have the deep brain stimulation put in, the trial panel noticed that the camera crew could be seen in the testing video, so I had to do all the tests again without the camera crew present.

The camera crew spent a few days with me, interviewing Andrew, me, and Mum. It was very intense. They also filmed Andrew shaving my head in preparation for the operation.

The night before my operation, I threw a bit of a party at home to celebrate life as I knew it. I wrote little notes to all the special people in my family who I wanted to encourage in case I did not pull through the operation.

As well as writing to my family, I also wrote what I wanted my end-of-life arrangements to be, and I gave them to my Pastor, sealed in an envelope. When I gave him the envelope and explained what was in it, he cried — oops!

I went to the hospital the night before my operation. On

the day of the operation, the camera crew, Mum, and Andrew came very early in the morning.

The operation went on for eight hours. A lot of work had to be done. I was just under enough anaesthetic that I do not remember anything, but awake enough to follow commands and answer questions.

I woke up in the ICU; Mum and Andrew came to visit, and I said, "Hello, Mum! Hello, Andrew!" They were like, "Yes! She remembers us!"

My recovery was speedy. On Friday, I had the internal part of my brain played with; the following Friday, I ate Macca's for breakfast at the plaza.

As I was part of a blind study, I did not know if the DBS device was turned on or turned off. Due to the swelling in the brain from the operation, the device felt like it was turned on. After about two weeks, I felt like my old self again.

Three months later, I saw Doctor Mahant, who changed my device. I had a terrible side effect to this. My left leg was in spasm, bent at the knee up around my ear. It was very uncomfortable and scary. I went to see Doctor Mahant again, but he could not do anything because it was a blind study. So, he assured me that I would be okay. To relax and go on my holiday. I did just that, and I was okay again.

Once the second lot of three months was over, I went to see Doctor Mahant, and he revealed that in the first three months, my device was turned off, and in the second lot of time, my device was turned on.

Upon discussing how I felt and what the doctors could see, the DBS had not done what the doctors hoped it would do, which was to eliminate all or most of the dystonic movements. Even though the trial was deemed 'unsuccessful,' it still made an impact on improving my disability as I was no longer holding my body tight, so I did not spasm. The DBS has relaxed my muscles, and I am more comfortable.

The fact that the DBS did work was proved every year

when I visited Doctor Mahant. He would turn off a bit of my DBS, and I could tell him what limb he had turned off because I would feel the muscles in that limb tighten again. He did not make any changes one year; I guessed nothing had changed. I have a one hundred percent record of guessing what Doctor Mahant has done in the testing!

After five years of using my device, I had to change the battery. It was a speedy operation, all of fifteen minutes. The operation was done in a day surgery unit of a nearby private hospital that was relatively new. I had to be at the hospital at 6am and I was home by noon.

The new battery was now rechargeable and would last ten years or more. I was given a charger that I placed on my battery to charge. I charged the battery every night, so it only took fifteen minutes instead of over one hour a week. I figured I would be better off if I got into a daily habit of charging.

The site of the incision in my chest healed differently from the first operation. It was very lumpy.

I was to see Doctor Mahant about four weeks after the battery change. Two days before this, I felt 'unwell' and it was getting harder to charge my device. When it came time to see Doctor Mahant, he took one look at me and ran out of the room. When he returned, he explained that I had to go directly to the hospital as I had some infection that was making its way to my brain.

He wrote me a letter to give to the hospital with two things that needed action.

One was to take some blood for a blood test. Two, I was to start taking some antibiotics.

Unfortunately, the order of things was reversed, and so the antibiotics hid what the infection was.

I stayed in the hospital for five days on intravenous antibiotics. To leave the hospital, I had to take two potent antibiotics at $200 a month, twice a day, that stripped my innards. I also had to have a blood test every fortnight to make sure the antibiotics were not destroying my kidneys and to see what level the infection was at. Having antibiotics half an hour before breakfast was murder! As soon as I had breakfast, I would have to go to the bathroom multiple times and lie down to recover. My GP was livid at what I had to go through.

After three months, I saw Doctor Mahant, and he said I could stop taking the antibiotics as the infection looked like it had been eliminated from my system.

A month later, the infection was back. The only option now was to operate and take out my device from my chest and a section of leads out of my neck to get rid of the foreign objects in my body to let my blood clear itself.

My surgeon was overseas and could not operate to remove part of my device, so Doctor Mahant found me a female surgeon. She was lovely, and I was happy she had performed my surgery. While I was in the hospital, I was on intravenous antibiotics again, but once I went home, I did not have to take anything.

It was strange not having my device. I felt an actual loss. It had helped me a lot, and now it was gone. I thought I could live without my device and get used to life as before, but I was wrong. Six weeks after I had part of my device removed, I went to see the surgeon again, and we made time to have surgery and put in a new battery and leads.

The surgeon was meticulous in operating, changing her gloves multiple times throughout the surgery.

I was infection-free and ready to do life again without seeing more hospitals. This was August 2015.

In October, the side of my head where the leads ran up did not feel right. I felt like I had a pimple on the side of my head. I had an upcoming appointment to see Doctor Mahant in November. When I saw him, he again freaked out and booked me in to see the surgeon straight away. When I saw the surgeon, she booked me in to swap my device from my right side to my left. The surgery took place a couple of days before Christmas.

I had to shave my head again.

The number of incisions that took place was numerous. Everything that had happened on the right side of my body had to also occur on the left side. I had stitches across the top of my head, behind my left and right ears, and on both sides of my chest.

After the surgery, the surgeon spoke to Andrew and explained that the wire behind my ear was a few layers of skin away from coming through and being exposed. Had the wire been exposed, the surgeon would have removed all my wires and electrodes.

I felt like I had dodged a bullet.

Christmas was enjoyable that year. My family had the biggest water balloon fight that I did not want to miss out on, but the stipulation by my mother was that I was not allowed to be hit. I did not throw any water balloons at anyone. I stealthily got balloons from the people who filled them up and handed them to the children so they had ammunition!

Once I had recovered from this surgery, I was alright on the DBS front. I was first given a prediction of ten years until my next battery change needed to take place, but eight years later, I have been told that it may stretch out to fourteen years, mainly because of how I take care of my battery. I still see Doctor Mahant every year.

Another area of my life where I am still working on setting boundaries is my fatigue. Mum was aware of my fatigue and gave me a slow-paced life. It was when I got married that I felt it the most. As I have gotten older, recovery from fatigue has taken longer. Now, I am only doing one big thing a day: taking a nap in the afternoon and not going out on consecutive days; this keeps my energy levels reasonable.

I have also noticed that if I have too much on my mind, I will feel tired to the point of not being able to function, getting anxiety attacks, and finding it hard to breathe. Life is a balance.

I think today, we are expected to do more and be more. I am making it my priority to listen to myself, eliminate the unnecessary, and do what feels right for me. Everything can seem urgent, but the question is, what is essential?

In Pursuit...

- Medicine is constantly improving.

- Some medicines can make you better; some can make you worse.

- It is all in the flip of a coin or the roll of a die.

My head is shaved and ready for my DBS operation

Chapter 15

Body Image

How does one perceive themselves in the world when no one looks like them? I do not mean in looks, but rather in image.

Growing up, I was always the one in the wheelchair with cerebral palsy. I have the rarest kind of cerebral palsy. Only ten percent of people with cerebral palsy have it. No one at my particular school had my form of cerebral palsy, and no one in my family has cerebral palsy.

Most importantly, no one in the media or on TV has ever had the cerebral palsy I have.

As an adult, I think it has become more confronting as we have access to social media twenty-four-seven.

It was only in my mid-thirties that I came across a group of neurologists who really understood me and could explain concisely why I could not walk; how my brain worked, or rather, did not work, and how the only way to improve any function would be to make medical changes in the brain. I had what I grew up believing was athetoid cerebral palsy. My new neurologist was now calling my condition dystonic cerebral palsy. This caused a bit of an identity crisis in me. Why had the name changed, and what did that mean? Athetoid was being used a bit too broadly, and they wanted to define the names of my movements to give them more meaning.

With medication, I move less, and with more moulded

seating, I can sit straight with both my feet on the footplates. At fifty years old, we have reached a significant position where I can sit straight with both feet on the footplates and remain relatively still.

Back to my body image. The media has gone mad, telling us we do not look good enough. We must look thinner, fitter, and stronger, eat better and healthier, and have fewer carbs and less sugar.

I went into my fifties feeling like my life was running out of control on a one-way ticket to fat.

I am still recovering from my coma. Waking up at forty-four kilos, trying to put on weight, to being the heaviest I have ever been three years later! My eating habits are better than before, but my lack of mobility is contributing to my weight gain. I am still working out how to move more in my head to make that happen physically, but it may take time. After all, everyone else is told to 'walk' and I cannot do that, so I will have to figure out something else to do instead of walking.

The real questions I want to answer are, 'What is health?' and 'What does healthy look like?' If I can put aside the media, who are just trying to make money in any way possible by body shaming and using scare tactics, I would answer in this way: Health is eating as well as you can, moving around as best as possible, and keeping good health in blood tests and blood pressure. Health comes in all shapes and sizes, and so it should. We are not robots; we cannot all look identical in shape and size. Our bodies are constantly changing, and we need to embrace this.

I have spoken to my GP and asked if I have anything to be concerned about. His reply was, "No." I cannot compare myself to people who walk around as my muscles and body fat are distributed differently throughout areas of my body.

I remember my sister, Esther, commenting to Mum that my body structure differed from theirs. Esther was not mean.

She was commenting on what she saw. My back is broader and has more muscle as my arms and back do all the heavy lifting. My buttocks and legs sit around and not do much most of the time. I might kick you occasionally, and I am sorry for that. I am either flexing my muscles or seeing if you are still awake.

Twenty percent of the population have some form of disability. Where are the standards of measure that tell me I am on the right track?

I would love for someone to show how a person in a wheelchair ages. What might happen to areas of our body, and what would be considered normal? Will my muscles stay tight around my waist, and my thighs grow like lava?

As I have become more involved in fashion, all the Pinterest photos I have ever seen are people modelling clothes standing up. I can honestly say that does not help. I need to see what the outfit looks like sitting down. If pants have pockets, I need to know if they bulge out the sides when you are sitting. It is what you are going to see on me all the time.

Recently, I joined an online course and asked if they had any photos of people sitting down in their clothes so I could visualise what the clothes would look like when you are sitting. They got back to me with some photos of people in wheelchairs looking great, and then I discovered there were more people on Pinterest modelling clothes in wheelchairs. The idea that there were photos on Pinterest had never occurred to me because there had been nothing for a long time.

I have been putting up photos of myself in my clothes on Facebook, Instagram, and YouTube to try and normalise the idea of being well-dressed in a wheelchair and getting dressed on a budget. The feedback I am getting is that people are inspired and motivated. I have also recently been given some hand-me-across clothes to try. The lady has always had great taste, and I was happy to receive them. Her clothes are beautiful, and I will share her generosity with others.

I think weight, body image, and fashion will always be a struggle for me, but I am going to try to accept who I am and always try my best to feel and look good.

In Pursuit...

- Healthy is when you eat well, move around, and do not notice what is expected of you in the media. Be well.

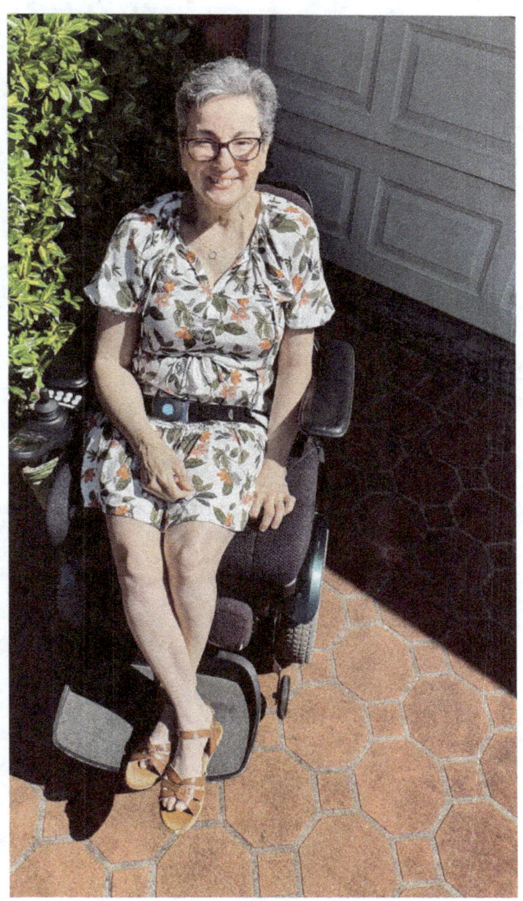

Me at forty-four kilograms

Me at sixty-plus kilograms

Chapter 16

Depression and Anxiety

Growing up, my parents both struggled with depression. Leaving their home country of Malta and moving to Australia meant they missed their family and friends. They no longer had their family support system or their social life.

I saw their loneliness from time to time. Mum would look sad and heavy. Dad would have bouts of anger and silence.

As a person with a disability, I first noticed a low mood in year six when girls were just horrible for the sake of it.

Again, when I was seventeen years old, I could not keep up with my schoolwork in year eleven. Once I left school, it took me a couple of months to get out of my low mood.

When my cousin, Scott, committed suicide, I felt sad, low, and lost. I could not make sense of his death. Back then, there was not much awareness about suicide. Society's take was that taking your own life was selfish, and the Catholic stand was that if you took your own life, you were going to hell.

I was not happy with either of these beliefs. I searched for a better answer as I needed to make peace with what suicide was. I attended workshops, watched what I could on TV, and read whatever I could get my hands on.

It took time — a lot of time — to figure out what suicide was. I have now made peace with the theory that the brain is not well due to an imbalance in serotonin that causes depression or anxiety. Facing more of life is unbearable, and wanting to die is what gives the person relief or hope.

More awareness, understanding, and better medications are available if people can get and receive the help.

I have watched both my sisters struggle with mental health issues. One refuses to take any medication. It has been awful to watch. My other sister, for years, needed medication and did not take anything. However, for the last couple of years, she has been on medication. Her life looks more manageable, and she is more pleasant to be around.

I remember when my sister was pregnant with her second child, a chemical imbalance occurred and my sister disappeared. Her body was there, but her spirit was gone. I missed her so much. I tried reaching out from time to time, but I could not reach her. It was like she was in a glass dome that I could not penetrate. Around the time my sister had her baby, I started going out with Andrew. About nine months after her baby was born, my sister came back. Her depression was gone. I remember introducing her to Andrew again and saying, "Andrew, this is my real sister. She's back!" She was very uncomfortable with this statement. My sister came back to her present self. She was smiling and laughing and hearing and responding comfortably. I could love her again. Not that I had stopped loving her; it was just that now I knew that she felt it.

I tried talking to her about what happened, but she became agitated and teary each time. It makes me sad.

My real depressive struggles have been around trying to have a baby. The chemicals in my brain changed when I heard that we would need to do IVF to conceive. Everything was beige for the first two years, and I had no taste. I was going through life in a haze.

I read an article on depression, and I could relate to most of the symptoms of depression. I told Andrew, "I have depression!" He said, "I know." I asked, "Why didn't you tell me and take me to the doctor?" He said, "I thought you knew." We went to the doctor the next day, and the medicine he gave me made me fearless. I was doing many things and trying new hobbies and colour was back in my life. The side effect of the medicine was that I was always hot, and I wore a tank top in winter and did not feel the cold.

I started seeing a new doctor, and I shared that I was constantly feeling hot on the medication I was on. The doctor changed my medication, and I felt better. I was no longer hot. The new medication just took the edge off my depression, and I was able to fight my way out of the rest. I could still feel all my emotions and cry when I needed to.

When I am depressed without medication, I will pick myself apart. I will keep telling myself that I have done this wrong and that wrong and that I have offended this person. No one should like me. I also have a continual loop of fantasies running through my mind. Sexual encounters or what I would do in this situation or that. It is exhausting.

The first time, I tried going off my medication it lasted a couple of months. I started ringing Mum and sharing my sadness and frustration with her, and it got a bit too much for her. My sister rang and asked me to sort myself out. I went back onto my medication.

I am unable to physically 'run' away from feelings. I imagine a run or a brisk walk is helpful for better mental health, but I cannot do that.

People with a disability are four times more likely to be susceptible to depression due to living in poverty and having less social contact.

A few support workers have shared with me that some of their clients just shut down and are in a trance-like state due to their depression. The trance-like state makes the client unable to communicate, and they go through the motions of their day. This may go on for months and is considered 'normal.'

I know that when I was living in Malta for nine months, I stopped thinking for myself because I did not have the freedom or the ability to go out on my own due to having no facilities for those with a disability. I was at the mercy of others to take me out.

Depression is mourning the loss of the past or unfulfilled dreams.

Anxiety is stressing over what is to come.

I experienced anxiety as a fear of going into new situations. As I write this, I can see that the first couple of years of high school were filled with anxiety. I feared every day. My fears were, "Am I going to make it to class on time? Are my friends going to want to help me? Can I keep up with the day?" Anxiety was not talked about much back in the eighties.

I had to work at removing the channel of fear from my mind as it was so ingrained. I cannot believe that it has taken me over thirty years to work out that the fear I felt every day for the first couple of years of high school was anxiety, huh?

Mental health is a health issue like heart disease and diabetes. When you are depressed, it is not an imaginary thing. You cannot just will yourself to get better. You may need to work with your thoughts via a psychologist or seek medical help via a GP.

My brother struggles with anxiety, and he gets agitated. We assure him that the situation will be okay, and it usually is, but it is sometimes excruciating to watch. My brother also has a brain injury. The brain injury brought on his anxiety in more extreme ways. I am constantly monitoring him, as other family members do not understand him. Most days, he does okay. Some days, I need to gently get information to him via email so he can take it in at his own pace. Talking to him overloads him.

After my coma, I was off my antidepressants for a couple of months, but as I saw my happiness slowly decline and the endless tapes start to creep back in, I thought it best to go back on my medication. I spoke to my GP about it, and he agreed.

In Pursuit...

- I want people to know that having a mental health issue, asking for help, and going on medication is being strong and brave, not weak.

Chapter 17

Better Than I Used to Be

I look back to where my journey began in this book. I was fighting for my life to get to my baseline of 'normal'. Learning how to navigate my body and mind has been a process. I was so weak in my body, and now, working slowly with my physiotherapist, exercise physiologist, and occupational therapist, I have almost returned to my baseline. I am in a better place, and I use my body safely.

My mind has also become stronger through this ordeal of recovering from being in a coma for sixty-seven days. I feel that past experiences of going through life as a disabled person and my battle with infertility prepared me for my struggle to recover from my coma.

Being determined and wanting to make my family proud of me by getting better and driving myself to be the best I can be is what drives me. In pursuit of normal!

Acknowledgments

I want to thank my husband, Andrew, for waking up early with me so I could finish my writing before the day began.

Thanks a million for waking up at those crazy early hours to prepare me for meeting with the Atmosphere Press team.

This book would not have happened without you, Sophie; thank you.

To my big, gigantic family: there is never a dull moment, and I'm glad you fight for me, encourage me, and love me. I love you all loads!

Thanks to my family and friends from all around the world who prayed for me while I was sleeping and at other times throughout my life.

Thanks to my editor, Tammy Letherer, for inspiring me to get my book over the finish line.

Thank you, Ronaldo Alves, for the fantastic cover design.

About Atmosphere Press

Founded in 2015, Atmosphere Press was built on the principles of Honesty, Transparency, Professionalism, Kindness, and Making Your Book Awesome. As an ethical and author-friendly hybrid press, we stay true to that founding mission today.

If you're a reader, enter our giveaway for a free book here:

SCAN TO ENTER
BOOK GIVEAWAY

If you're a writer, submit your manuscript for consideration here:

SCAN TO SUBMIT
MANUSCRIPT

And always feel free to visit Atmosphere Press and our authors online at atmospherepress.com. See you there soon!

About the Author

MARTHA SIEDE lives with her husband, Andrew, and her dog, Bronte, at the foot of the Blue Mountains in Western Sydney, Australia. Martha's passion is to show others that anything is possible if you are determined to improve and reach your goals. Martha loves encouraging people to pursue their dreams. Martha has a wicked sense of humour and enjoys making people laugh. This is the first book Martha has written.

InPursuitOfNormal@gmail.com

www.ingramcontent.com/pod-product-compliance
Lightning Source LLC
Chambersburg PA
CBHW071516140726
47997CB00005B/1987